# LIFE
# UNDER
# THE
# PHARAOHS

**By the same author:**

ALL MEN ARE NEIGHBOURS
MADAME TUSSAUD
ONE MAN'S JOURNEY
THE MOUNTAINS OF PHARAOH
THE ANVIL OF CIVILISATION
SEEING ROMAN BRITAIN
LOST CITIES
THE BULL OF MINOS
WONDERS OF THE WORLD
LIFE UNDER THE PHARAOHS

# LIFE
# UNDER
# THE
# PHARAOHS

by
LEONARD COTTRELL

HOLT, RINEHART AND WINSTON
New York

FIRST EDITION

Library of Congress Catalog Card Number: 60-13042

81580—0410

Printed in the United States of America

To
SIR ALAN GARDINER
in appreciation of a valued friendship

# ACKNOWLEDGMENTS

The author and publishers are indebted to the following for quotations made in this book:

Constable & Co., Ltd., for the extracts from Petrie's *Social Life in Ancient Egypt*; J. M. Dent & Sons, Ltd., for the extracts from the Everyman Edition of *History* by Herodotus; Egypt Exploration Society for the quotations from R. O. Faulkner's article, "Egyptian Military Organisation"; John Farquharson, Ltd., for an Egyptian song from *The Glory of the Pharaohs* by Arthur Weigall; Fouad University Press for the quotations from the writings of Dr. P. C. Sobhy Bey; Macmillan & Co., Ltd., for the extracts from Erman's *Life in Ancient Egypt*; Methuen & Co., Ltd., for the extracts from Erman's *The Literature of the Ancient Egyptians*; The Metropolitan Museum of Art for the quotation from *The Tomb of Rekh-mi-Re*; The Clarendon Press for the extracts from *The Legacy of Egypt*; Sampson Low, Marston Co., Ltd., for the extract from *Everyday Life in Ancient Egypt*, by A. W. Shorter; Sidgwick and Jackson for the quotation from Margaret Murray's *The Splendour That Was Egypt*; The University of Chicago Press for the quotation from *The Intellectual Adventure of Ancient Man*, by Frankfort, Wilson and Jacobsen, published in Great Britain under the title, *Before Philosophy*.

The author is also grateful to the following for the use of photographs to supplement his own collection: B. O. A. C.; Mrs. R. Engelbach; Lehnert & Landrock, Cairo; British Museum; Ashmolean Museum.

# INTRODUCTION

A number of specialized works have been written by professional Egyptologists on the everyday life of the Ancient Egyptians, though many of these are now out of print. I am not a specialist, and I would not be so presumptuous as to attempt to write a comprehensive textbook on Egyptian life and culture, for which task others are far better qualified than I. In any case, I must say frankly that not every aspect of this ancient civilization attracts me equally, and readers who want, for example, a fully documented account of Egyptian law and administration or military organization can find these dealt with in the more specialized works to which I have referred, and which are listed in the Bibliography at the end of this book.

Broadly speaking, this book deals with the daily life of the Pharaoh's people, the houses they lived in, the dress they wore, how they amused themselves, with chapters on such subjects as the life of women and children, of the soldier, the scribe, the doctor, the craftsman, and the great administrator. But in choosing my subjects I have been guided mainly by my own preferences and enthusiasms, for only in this way could I give the book life. Therefore, as far as possible, each chapter has been linked with some scene or object, the sculptured head of a woman, a child's toy, a painted scene in an Egyptian tomb, a poem, a story, or even some modern parallel with the life of the ancient people which I have observed among the modern *fellahin*.

These personal memories of things which have moved or intrigued me provide the springboards for my various chapters.

Even so, it seemed to me that a book about people *en masse* stood in grave danger of boring the general reader. I therefore went a step further and between each chapter of factual information I inserted other chapters in which I have tried to create a group of characters, the Vizier Rekhmire, and his family and friends, and to set them in motion against their native surroundings. Although some (though not all) of their activities are fictitious, all could have happened; the Vizier and his wife Meryet were real persons and their tomb still remains in the Theban Necropolis. Readers who are curious to know how much is real and how much imagined will find the answers in the Appendix, "Fact or Fiction?"

Many years ago I came across a passage in a book by Arthur Weigall, an Egyptologist who never wrote a dull line, and which I will take the liberty of quoting because it sums up my own approach to the study of the ancient world:

A man has no more right to think of the people of old as dust than he has to think of his contemporaries as lumps of meat. The true archaeologist does not take pleasure in skeletons as skeletons, for his whole effort is to cover them decently with flesh and skin once more, and to put some thoughts back in the empty skulls. Nor does he delight in ruined buildings because they are ruined buildings; rather he deplores that they are ruined. . . . In fact, the archaeologist is so enamoured of life that he would raise all the dead from their graves. He will not have it that the men of old are dust; he would bring them forth to share with him the sunlight which he finds so precious. He is such an enemy of Death and Decay that he would rob them of their harvest; and for every life that the foe has claimed he would raise up, if he could, a memory that would continue to live.

LEONARD COTTRELL.

# CONTENTS

*Page*

# CHAPTER 1

# THE LAND, THE PEOPLE, AND THEIR GODS

IT is an old truism that a people's character is formed by the land and the climate in which it lives. If this is true of people like the English, who have occupied their country for less than fifteen hundred years, or the Americans, who have been settled in their vast continent for only a few generations, how much more true it is of the Egyptians, who have lived in their narrow, desert-bounded valley for more than six thousand years! Also, whereas other countries have changed and developed over the centuries, losing much of their original character, Egypt has not. The same conditions which governed the lives of the millions who lived under the Pharaohs still largely apply today. Therefore, before one can attempt to describe the people, it is necessary to present a picture, however sketchy, of this extraordinary country, the like of which exists nowhere else in the world.

Not long ago I was lying in my berth in a *wagon-lit*, trundling through the night along the four hundred-odd miles which separate Luxor, in Upper Egypt, from Cairo. A few days before I had traveled up to Luxor by day, a journey which took ten hours. The view from the train windows was a monotonous, never-ending panorama of cotton fields, sugar plantations, mud-brick villages, palm trees—always with the brown desert hills to right and left, sometimes coming close, at other times retreating into the distance, but never absent from view. It was like watching a travel film endlessly repeated.

But there is something about the night journey which always stirs my imagination—I do not quite know why. The train rumbles and rocks, the rapid puffing of the locomotive roars in the ventilators, and as one lies comfortably in one's bunk, pictures form in the mind.

I imagined some watcher from the skies, a sky-deity, looking down on this green serpent, the Nile Valley, coiling through the desert waste for six hundred miles and more, never more than a few miles wide and often less than a mile in width. On the west, stretches an endless waste of sand and rock—the Sahara. On the other side the Arabian Desert rolls eastward for hundreds of miles until it reaches the Red Sea. There is a full moon and my sky-god would see the great river shining like pale silver. Here and there he would see a sprinkling of lights along the banks—towns like Keneh, and Asuit, and Ballana. But he would not see the hundreds of unlighted villages where the millions of *fellahin* sleep the sleep of exhaustion, huddled in their mud-brick villages, until the sun calls them out to the flat fields to continue their eternal labors.

To how many millions of human souls has this green snake given birth during the past hundred centuries? As an Immortal, my sky-god would remember the time before man was known in the valley, when the green gash in the desert was known only to animals, birds, and reptiles; when lions and hyenas, cheetahs and wolves roamed the desert fringes, and hippopotami splashed in the water; when huge flocks of geese rose above the papyrus marshes in clouds.

My god would have seen how, century after century, the jungle gave way to cultivation. He would have seen for the first time on this planet ordered cities developing, surrounded by fields, threaded by roads and canals, while the rest of the human race, or most of it, still wandered from hunting ground to hunting ground—barbarians whose only skill was in killing animals to maintain a mere existence.

Later, some forty-five hundred years ago, he would have seen the pyramids rising, sprinkled like a child's building blocks along thirty miles of the western bank, the eternal homes of kings who wanted to be gods. He would see the great city of Memphis with its palaces, temples, and gardens, and other towns scattered along the valley from the Delta to the Nubian frontier. Fifteen centuries later he would have seen Thebes, the Imperial City, rising stately under the hacked ridges of the Theban hills. If he had peered low enough, he might have caught the gleam of the Pharaoh's golden war chariots and the dust rising behind the columns of his marching soldiers, moving southward to punish the Nubians, or northeastward to do battle with the Hittites.

He would remember the Cretan ships moving up the Nile to Thebes, bearing gifts for the Pharaoh; and later, ships of a different sort, manned by the fierce men of Macedonia, led by the generals of Alexander the Great. He saw the coming of the Romans, watched Hadrian's legionaries camping beside the colossi of Memnon at Luxor, where the soldiers pottered about among the thousand-

year-old tombs, and scrawled initials on the walls just as
the tourists of the nineteenth century used to do.

The armies of the Prophet with their horses and ban-
ners, the Turks, the armies of Napoleon, Nelson's fleet at
Aboukir, Gordon marching south to his death at Khartoum,
the flash of the guns before Alamein—all these he would
have seen. And now he would mark a train crawling north-
ward beside the winding river, a red glow followed by a
string of lights.

I think that is why this journey, which I have made
several times, will never lose its fascination for me. When
you take the train from Luxor to Cairo, you travel in ten
hours through more than half the history of mankind.

There, then, is the land; narrow, constricted, hemmed
in by its inhospitable deserts, but fertilized everlastingly
by the mud brought down each year by the flooding Nile.
For more than three thousand years before the birth of
Christ the oldest civilization on earth flourished in that
narrow valley. The pyramids, the tombs, the temples and
obelisks speak of the power of its kings, the mysteries of its
religion, and the richness of its culture. Also, because of
their passionate love of this life and their anxiety that it
should continue in the afterworld, the wealthier Egyptians
have left, in their tombs, paintings and sculptures which
vividly illustrate the occupations, pursuits, and pleasures
which they enjoyed in this life, and which they ardently
wished to continue in the next.

They have also left us many examples of their furniture, their dress, models of their houses, their weapons of
war, their boats, their games and amusements, and docu-

ments which range from official histories, religious texts and business transactions to school exercises, poems, and romances.

And yet for all this the Egyptians remain for most of us a mysterious race of people. This is partly due to the fact that until about 125 years ago, when the hieroglyphs began to be deciphered, they *were* mysterious—a people who had left monuments, sculptures, and paintings, but whose language was unknown. It is true that classical historians and travelers like Herodotus, Pliny, and Diodorus Siculus had left records of their travels in Egypt, but these tended only to strengthen the legend. For if the religious and other customs which Herodotus described seemed strange to him, how much stranger they must have appeared to the nineteenth-century historians! And even when the hieroglyphs were imperfectly translated, the bulk of records and inscriptions seemed to be concerned, not with warm-blooded human beings like ourselves, who made love, bore and brought up children, followed careers, enjoyed sports and pastimes. Instead, there were records of a morbid, melancholy race, perpetually obsessed with death; a people whose religion seemed a hotchpotch of magic and superstition, of animal-headed gods and monsters which, unlike the Greek gods and goddesses, hadn't even the merit of possessing human qualities like our own.

This, as we know now, was a libel on the Ancient Egyptians, who, like their modern descendants, seem to have been an extremely cheerful, life-loving people, but it is not difficult to see how they acquired their undeserved reputation for gloom and mystery. First, they had a fervent hope for an afterlife, which for all except their god-kings was to be very like this one. In order to enjoy this afterlife, they thought it necessary to build for themselves, if they could afford it, an "Eternal Habitation"—a tomb which would last for eternity—and to place within it, either in actuality or representation, the articles they would need to make life comfortable and happy. These included their clothes, their furniture, and household goods, the boats in which they would travel along the heavenly Nile, their hunting weapons with which they would spear fish or catch wildfowl, and representations, either statues or wall reliefs, of the servants who would minister to them after death as they had in life. It is this materialistic attitude towards death which has left us the legacy of beautiful or curious objects which are scattered throughout the museums of the world.

Second, whereas their homes were built of perishable material, usually mud-brick and timber, which have disappeared, their tombs were built to last forever and have therefore survived. The same is true of the great temples which were the homes of their gods. The colossal temple of Amun at Karnak, with its 70-foot drum columns and massive pylons, remains to awe and astonish us; but the palaces of the kings, the mansions of the nobles with their courts and gardens, and the million dwellings of lesser men have largely disappeared. The result is that when we visit Egypt, we see either tombs or religious buildings, or if we visit our local museum, we find that most of the objects on view have either a religious or funerary significance. It is as if a visitor coming to Britain or America three thousand years hence should find nothing remaining but churches and cemeteries. Such a visitor might be excused for imagining that we had spent most of our time in the worship of God or the care of our dead, but he would be wrong.

Similarly with Egypt; the work of hundreds of scholars—philologists poring over papyri, excavators discovering tombs or sifting among the scanty remains of ancient towns, students laboriously copying and photographing tomb paintings—has produced a wealth of human material which proves that the Ancient Egyptians had other occupations and interests besides worshiping their gods or preparing for the next world. It is from this material, and from my own observations, that I hope to paint a picture of ancient Egyptian life: in camps and courts, on the farms, in the law courts and temples, and not least in the home. But there are certain difficulties and dangers of which the reader should be warned in advance.

The first is a fairly obvious one: the fact that the period of Egyptian history with which we are to deal covers over three thousand years, a period three times as long as that which separates us from Alfred the Great. One has only to reflect on the changes which have occurred in English manners and customs in half that time to understand the difficulty of describing the life of a people over thirty centuries. To take each phase of Egyptian history in turn and describe the evolution of dress and furniture alone would require several books of this size. However, the writer (and the reader) can take comfort from the fact that the Ancient Egyptians were a very conservative people, and although important changes in dress and manners did take place over that enormous period of time, certain basic elements did not alter. Even during the time of the Ptolemies, in the third century B.C., art and architecture,

19

dress and religious observances bore, to the untutored eye, a very close resemblance to those of the pyramid builders, who lived more than two thousand years earlier. Even to-day the pattern of agricultural life in Egypt is not unlike what it was in Pharaonic times. From the train which carried me to Luxor I saw peasants digging the furrows with hoes exactly like those shown on the shoulders of the *shawabti* figures,[1] and in a Delta village I examined primitive beehives of mud-brick, shaped like a drainpipe, which the Ancient Egyptians also used. Even the musical instruments with which the *fellah* amuses himself in his few hours of leisure are like those depicted in the Theban tomb paintings.

However, to avoid confusion, I shall be careful to state from which particular period of Egyptian history—the Old, Middle, or New Kingdoms—my illustrations are drawn, and for those who are not familiar with these divisions there is a Dynastic table at the end of this book.

The second difficulty, to which I drew attention above, is more subtle and dangerous. It is the danger that, because the Ancient Egyptians were human beings like ourselves, with the same passions, appetites, and failings, because they sat on chairs, slept on beds, sent their children to school or their sons into the army, we may grow to think that they were more like us than they really were. True, human nature has changed remarkably little in five thousand years, but, civilized though the Egyptians undoubtedly were, the gap which separated them from primitive beliefs was much narrower than it is with us. Their religion, though it had

[1] Funerary statuettes of servants left in Ancient Egyptian tombs to serve their masters in the afterworld.

an ethical content, was full of animism and magic, survivals of the not-so-distant days before the first civilization grew up along the Nile Valley. In that world the savage ancestors of the Ancient Egyptians lived in fear, surrounded by hostile forces which had to be outwitted by magic or placated by blood-sacrifice.

To say that their religion dominated their lives is probably an exaggeration, but it certainly played a much more important part in their daily lives than does the religion of most Occidental peoples. Unless we recognize this, unless we make the effort of imagination needed to enter into their minds, we shall never understand them. Therefore, before I begin my close-ups of individual aspects of Egyptian life I would like to sketch in this fundamental, ever-present background of religious belief.

There is an excellent, recently published book, *The Intellectual Adventure of Ancient Man,* by Frankfort, Wilson, and Jacobsen, which is a great help in understanding this background, and I will take the liberty of quoting from it. After pointing out the isolation of Ancient Egypt, with its high population concentrated in the narrow valley of the Nile, the authors say:

> The two features of isolation and semi-urban population combine to make Egypt different from her neighbours. . . .
>
> The Egyptians are not subject to the great conservative control of the Arabian Desert. The deserts adjacent to Palestine are potential breeding-grounds for fierce and puritanical elements in the population of those countries. Egypt, with her agricultural wealth

and with her people living cheek by jowl, developed an early sophistication, which expressed itself intellectually towards catholicity and syncretism. Within Egypt the most divergent concepts were tolerantly accepted and woven together into what we moderns might regard as a clashing philosophical lack of system, but which to the ancient was *inclusive*. The way of the Semite, who held contact with the desert, was to cling fiercely to tradition and resist innovations, which changed the purity and simplicity of life. The way of the Egyptian was to accept innovations and incorporate them into his thought *without discarding the old and outmoded*. [Our italics.] Old and new link blandly together like some surrealist picture of youth and age on a single face.

Just how complex the religion was may be judged by the fact that scholars have identified two thousand separate deities in the Egyptian pantheon. Before Egypt became a unified state at the beginning of the First Dynasty (3200 B.C.), the Nile Valley was inhabited by hundreds of separate tribes, each of which had its own local deity. Of these, some were deified chieftains; some were animals, reptiles or birds; others were tree spirits or totems. After unification, which was first accomplished by King Menes, the god of the town or province from which the ruling family came usually became the chief or "state" god. For instance, in the Old Kingdom (2780–2100 B.C.)—the age of the pyramid-builders, the state god was the solar deity Re, whose worship centered at Heliopolis, not far from the capital of Memphis. Much later, when a Theban family ruled Egypt, Amun, the god of Thebes, shared pride of place with Re; in fact the two became identified under the name Amun-Re, "King of the Gods." But this did not mean that the hundreds of local godlings were discarded. They continued to be worshiped in their districts, and were absorbed by the systematizing priesthood in a complex theological system which must have been almost as bewildering to the ordinary Egyptian as it is to us.

In the Middle Kingdom (2100 to 1700 B.C.) the most important religious development was the rise of the Osiris cult which continued to be practiced right down to the Roman period, and which probably had more influence over the mass of the people than Amun-Re. The following brief account of the cult, which I quote from my book, *The Lost Pharaohs,* may be useful in helping to understand the part which the legend of Isis and Osiris played in the everyday life of the Ancient Egyptians:

Like most primitive peoples the ancestors of the Ancient Egyptians had their folk-myths which explained the origin of the world. They believed that in the beginning only the ocean existed, and on this ocean appeared an egg (in some versions a flower) from which was born the sun-god. He had four children, Geb and Shu, Tefnut and Nut. Planting their feet on Geb, Shu and Tefnut raised their sister Nut to the heavens. Thus Geb became the earth, Shu and Tefnut the atmosphere, and Nut the sky. Geb and Nut had four children, Osiris and Isis, Nepthys and Seth. Osiris succeeded to the throne of his father and governed the world wisely and justly, aided by his sister Isis,

23

whom he married. Seth, jealous of his brother's power, plotted to destroy him and eventually succeeded, afterwards cutting the body of Osiris into pieces which he buried in several parts of Egypt. The head was buried at Abydos. The faithful Isis recovered the scattered fragments of her husband's corpse, and with the aid of the jackal-god Anubis, who subsequently became the god of embalmment, re-animated it. Though unable to return to his life on earth, Osiris passed to the Underworld, where he became the god of the dead and later the judge of souls. Isis bore a son, Horus, who afterwards took revenge on his uncle, Seth, defeating the usurper in battle and winning back his father's throne.

The legend became the most popular of all Egyptian folk-myths. It never lost its hold on the people, because of its human appeal, Isis becoming the type of loyal wife and mother; Horus, the ideal son. In the Middle Kingdom it developed into the leading cult, and Abydos, supposed burial-place of the head of Osiris, became a place of pilgrimage. Every year thousands flocked to Abydos to watch a dramatic re-enactment of scenes in the life of Osiris, and to follow the procession of the God's body to his supposed tomb. Abydos thus became one of the most sacred places in Egypt. Noble families sought burial there, and others, who could not afford a tomb, erected memorial tablets in the hope that the God of the Dead would remember their names. It was during the "Middle Kingdom" that the conception of Osiris as a *judge of souls* became predominant, and for the first time the idea of accountability in the after-life for sins committed on earth began to take hold of the human mind.

Comparisons have been drawn between the Osiris cult and Christianity, and some of the resemblances are striking. Isis, the mother-goddess, is frequently shown with the infant Horus in her arms, as Mary is shown with the infant Jesus. Also Osiris was a god of resurrection, and in many tombs archaeologists have found wooden trays containing corn seeds, cut out in the form of the god, the corn symbolizing the renewal of life. Similarly, when a man died, he became "an Osiris" and was represented in the tomb paintings in the form of the mummified god.

Though the complexities of the higher Egyptian theology probably meant nothing to the mass of the people who were allowed only in the precincts of the great temples of Amun-Re, the state god, it is important to remember that these and other lesser deities were nevertheless woven into the lives of the common people. In every museum and antique shop in the world you will find tiny bronze and faïence statuettes of Amun-Re; of Isis and Osiris; of Hathor, goddess of love and beauty; of fat little Bes, the god of music and dancing, and hundreds of others. These were the daily companions of the people, occupying the same honored place in Egyptian homes as do the statuettes of Christ and His saints in millions of Christian homes today. Similarly, an Egyptian mother probably taught her children the stories of Isis, the good wife and mother, of Horus, the good son, and Seth, the wicked god, in much the same way that Christian mothers teach their children the stories of the Bible.

But there is an important difference, which it is well to remember in order to avoid falling into the trap against which I warned earlier in this chapter: the error of too closely identifying the Ancient Egyptian mind with our own. It is not difficult to draw parallels between the Osiris cult and Christianity, because the former is the most spiritual of the Egyptian cults and embodies moral attitudes which we can understand. Evil is punished and good triumphs. The wronged and suffering God is saved by his sister-wife, is restored to life and becomes the judge of souls, while his son wreaks vengeance on the evildoer. But when we come to consider the other deities, the modern mind meets with difficulties.

I can best illustrate them by asking the reader to consider first the personalities of the Old and New Testaments; second, the Greek and Roman deities; and, third, a typical group of gods and goddesses of Ancient Egypt.

In the first example, all the people involved, save One, are human beings. Some are prophets, divinely inspired; some are saints and martyrs. But all are undoubtedly human, even if some of them have spiritual qualities which transcend ours. In the second case we are dealing with supernatural beings—Zeus, the King of gods; Poseidon, the god of the ocean; Aphrodite, the goddess of love; Ares, the god of war, and so on. But though they are immortals endowed with superhuman powers they are still recognizably human; they have human forms and human frailties.

Now look at a typical frieze representing some of the deities of the Egyptian pantheon. Here is a god with the body of a man and the head of a jackal. Here is another with the head of a ram. Beside him stands a woman with the head of a lioness, and not far away crouches a crocodile; but he is a god, too. So is the cow which stands nearby, while the figure of the king crouches below, sucking milk from her udders. She is Hathor, who in one of her aspects is the Egyptian goddess of love.

It is this which baffles our modern Western minds. Here was a people whose buildings, statuary, and paintings still astonish the world; a people which built the pyramids and the Karnak Temple. They understood astronomy and were capable of precise geometrical calculation. They practiced medicine and surgery. They had a highly organized civil administration; they conquered and administered an Empire which at one time stretched from the Sudan to the Euphrates. And they developed an elaborate system of writing and had a reputation for wisdom which even the Greeks acknowledged. Yet these same people worshiped and mummified cats and snakes, and had as one of their principal gods a bull which, after being worshiped in life, was embalmed upon death, adorned with gold like a king, and ceremonially buried in a huge rock-cut sepulcher specially made for the purpose.

Nor were the Egyptians alone in this. The Minoans of Crete, the Assyrians, and Babylonians, also highly developed peoples, practiced animal cults as strange as this. And not only were animals worshiped; there were sacred stones, sacred trees, sacred pillars.

Here is the gulf which separates us from the men and women of those early civilizations. It is a gulf which, perhaps, can never be completely bridged, but with a little imagination and knowledge we can go a long way to meet them. The anthropologist who has studied the habits of primitive man in the modern world can help us. Here, for instance, is a useful thought from *The Intellectual Adventures of Ancient Man,* from which I have already quoted:

> The fundamental difference between the attitudes of modern and ancient man as regards the surrounding world is this; for modern, scientific man the phenomenal world is primarily an "It." For ancient— and also for primitive—man it is "Thou. . . ." An object, an "It" can always be scientifically related to other objects and appear as part of a group or series. In this manner science insists on seeing "It," hence science is able to comprehend objects and events as ruled by universal laws which make their behaviour under given circumstances predictable. "Thou" has the unprecedented, unparalleled, and unpredictable character of an individual, a presence known only in so far as it reveals itself. . . . For these reasons there is justification for the aphorism of Crawley: "Primitive man has only one mode of thought, one mode of expression, one part of speech—*the personal.*" This does not mean (as is often thought) that primitive man, in order to explain natural phenomena, imparts human characteristics to an inanimate world. *Primitive man simply does not know an inanimate world.* [Our italics.]
>
> For this very reason he does not "personify" the inanimate phenomena nor does he fill an empty world with the ghosts of the dead, as "animism"

would have us believe. The world appears to primitive man neither inanimate nor empty but abundant with life; and life has individuality, in man or beast or plant, and in every phenomena which confronts man —the thunderclap, the sudden shower, the eerie unknown clearing in the wood, the stone which suddenly hurts him when he stumbles while on a hunting trip. Any phenomenon may at any time face him, not as "It" but as "Thou."

The Ancient Egyptians, though a highly civilized people, were much nearer to primitive man than we are, and their attitude towards their natural surroundings, towards the animal world, and towards what we now call "the forces of Nature" can best be understood within the framework of this "Thou" relationship. Then it is easier to understand why they deified animals.

The falcon floating in the sky with no more apparent motive power than the sun; the jackal flitting ghostlike along the margin of the desert; the crocodile lurking lump-like on the mud-flats; or the powerful bull in whom was the seed of procreation. These beasts were forces going beyond the normality of the landscape; they were forces which transcended the minimal observed natures of animals. They therefore took on high relief in the scene and were believed to be vested with mysterious or inscrutable forces related to an extra-human world.[2]

[2] Frankfort, Wilson and Jacobsen, *The Intellectual Adventure of Ancient Man.*

To put it in another way: before science showed mechanism which animates plants and animals, before man knew that animals, reptiles, and birds were of a lower species but kindred to himself, *he could only judge them in relation to his own humanity.* What interested and awed him was the fact that they were so different from himself and that they possessed powers and functions which he had not. The bird with its power of flight; the lion with its immense strength; the crocodile which lurked in the river and could take off a man's leg with a snap of its jaws; the snake with its secret, silent, furtive life; and the ibis with its dignified air of wisdom. He did not catch these animals and study them in zoos; he respected and revered them because they possessed superhuman powers. And therefore, in time, the flying falcon became the one of the insignia of royalty; the crocodile an infernal monster which devoured guilty souls. The ibis became Thoth, the god of wisdom (and of writing), and the lion, as the Sphinx, symbolized kingly majesty.

Remember also that the Egyptian in his narrow valley lived far closer to animals than we do. Crocodiles and hippopotami swarmed in the river, huge flocks of geese lived in the papyrus marshes, falcons hovered in the sky. If we bear these facts in mind, we shall be able to understand better the mysterious, and to us sometimes grotesque, aspects of the religion which was the ever-present background of the Egyptian's daily life.

# CHAPTER 2

# REKHMIRE COMES HOME

MY aim is to get as close as possible to the daily life of the Ancient Egyptians. I have said something about their land and the gods they worshiped. If this were a classified textbook, with each aspect of Egyptian life neatly tabulated under headings, this chapter would be headed "Law and Administration" or "How They Were Governed." It is important that these matters should be understood, but it is even more important that the human beings whom we wish to meet should not be lost in a welter of facts concerning taxation, land and property dues, the legal system, and the machinery of government. I was reflecting on how best to deal with these subjects when I happened to come across a picture of a boat. It shows one of the beautiful ships of which numerous models exist in the Egyptian Museum at Cairo, in the British Museum and other collections; it is reproduced on Plate 5.

For the Egyptian the boat was the principal means of transport, and as the Nile played such an important part in his life, he had every reason to expect that much of his traveling in the afterlife would also be by water. So he buried these model boats in his tomb. Such boats have always fascinated me. If you look carefully at this model, you will see what a delightful craft it was, with the curving hull, the benches for the rowers, the mast and big square sail, and amidships a cabin for the owner, roofed against the fierce Egyptian sunlight but open at the sides to admit the breeze. It was in vessels such as these that the Pharaoh, and his ministers and high officials made their journeys along the Nile, and sometimes along the Syrian coast to visit their colonies. In some of the cabins you will see a tiny effigy of the owner; even his cabin trunk is included, stowed away under his bunk.

This boat gave me an idea. It was part of the duties of high officials of Pharaoh to make periodical tours of the provinces on behalf of their royal master, visiting local governors, or *nomarchs* (the provinces were called *nomes*) to investigate matters concerning taxation—and particularly to check extortion—to study the state of the land and the irrigation canals, to inspect garrisons, or to settle legal disputes. An official's functions varied according to the position he held.

Let us imagine that we are traveling through Egypt in the boat of one of these high officials. The period is that of the Eighteenth Dynasty (1555–1350 B.C.) in the reign of Tuthmosis III. We are traveling in the boat of the Vizier Rekhmire. This man actually existed. His tomb is one of the most interesting to be seen in Thebes, and although this journey is imaginary, it is one he could very easily have made. The duties he performed, which will be described as the journey proceeds, are set out in detail on the walls of his tomb.

Before we start, a word about the functions of the Vizier. He was the chief officer of state under the Pharaoh. He carried into effect all the administrative side of the royal functions, apart from the religious aspect (for the

Pharaoh was also the Chief Priest). He appointed the four
"reporters" who were responsible, three times a year, for a
statement on the affairs of the provinces. He received the
reports of the District Inspectors; he attended to provincial
boundaries, allocations of land, orders for second crops,
inundation, tax arrears, robberies in the provinces, and the
complaints of local governors.

Under him were many other officials whose high-
sounding titles are inscribed in their tombs: "The Fanbearer at the King's right hand"; "The Eyes and Ears of
the King," who made confidential inquiries; "The Messenger in the Country, who filled the heart of the King"; the
tutor, "making excellent of the King"; the "Scribe of
Horus the strong bull" (*i.e.*, the King); the "Chief of the
Guard"; and many others. It is likely that some of these
officials might be traveling with the Vizier. We may imagine, then, a small flotilla of boats moving up the river
from the Delta to Thebes, the imperial capital.

The Vizier and his staff have been on a visit to some of
the Syrian coast towns which owe allegiance to Pharaoh, for
at this time, thanks to the conquests of Tuthmosis III, the
Egyptians control a large part of what is now Syria, Israel,
and the Lebanon. Running southward before the wind,
with the mountainous Mediterranean coast away to our
left, we come at last to the coast of Egypt. Long before we
see the shore, the blue sea is stained with brown mud, which
becomes denser as we approach the mouth of the great
river. Then we see the long, flat coastline; the palm trees
and the acacias; and the wide, green expanse of the Nile
Delta.

Shortly after our boat enters one of the two main

33

branches of the Nile the wind drops. The rowers curse under their breath, for this means that they will have to unship their oars and begin the long, hard pull upstream. But the Vizier is a great man, and an impatient one. He has much to see and do before he can arrive at his home in Thebes. So there is nothing for it but to start rowing. Down comes the big square sail. It is furled along the yard. The brown-skinned sailors, naked to the waist, bend their backs; the oars creak in steady rhythm; and from a platform near the stern the gong sends out its brazen notes, keeping time for the rowers. One of the men raises his voice in a monotonous chant, and with each pull at the oars the sailors sing a refrain. The brown water rushes past the long, curving hull and high up in the stern the steersman manipulates the huge steering paddles, watching out for sand-banks, and occasionally shouting a greeting, or an insult, to the steersmen of passing craft.

Under an awning amidships sits the Vizier, dictating to his scribes. He wears a long white robe of fluted linen, and a heavy black wig frames a face of great dignity. His scribes, who sit before him cross-legged, their rolls of papyrus on their knees, are more simply dressed in short white kilts. Ahead, on the poop, stands the captain, giving orders to the crew. Behind the Vizier's ship follow the other boats of the flotilla, their flashing oar blades catching the gleam of the sun.

Only the Vizier and his high officials wear wigs. The crew is shaven-headed, and all of them wear the simple white kilt, leaving the breast bare. Fifteen hundred years ago, in the time of the Old Kingdom, when the Pyramids

were built, even noblemen wore the kilt, but in these days
men of rank have taken to the long robe. But there is
one thing which all have in common. They are all clean-
shaven. That is why it is easy to distinguish an Asiatic ship
when it passes. Here comes one now, moving rapidly down-
stream, its cargo piled high on the deck. Even if they had
not noticed its foreign rig, our crew would have known
that the ship was not Egyptian, for its crew are bearded.
Our men look curiously at it and the foreigners look back
at us. As the two vessels pass abreast, our captain sings out
a greeting in a language which is not Egyptian and the
foreign captain replies in the same tongue. The strangers
are Syrians.

In the time of the Old Kingdom the Egyptians knew
little of the world outside their own valley, but now, in the
New Kingdom, they have moved out to conquer an Empire.
Tuthmosis III, the greatest of the warrior Pharaohs, has
led his armies as far as the Euphrates in the northeast, and
has subdued the Nubians in the south. Foreign captives
have been brought back to Thebes; foreign princes are
being brought up at the Pharaoh's court; and some Egyptian noblemen have married foreign wives. Nor have these
contacts been achieved entirely by conquest. The Pharaoh
has diplomatic and commercial relations with other powers:
with the Hittite Empire, with the Kings of Babylon, and
the rulers of the great maritime empire of Crete. Rekhmire
knows these people well, and in his tomb, which is already
in preparation in the Theban necropolis, his artists have
depicted him receiving gifts from the "Sea-people," as the
islanders were known to the Egyptians. Even now, as we

35

round a bend in the river, another foreign ship comes into view, and one of Rekhmire's staff draws his attention to it. "The *Keftiu*," he says. (See Plate 45.)

As the two ships pass, the Vizier makes a courteous bow towards the Cretan official who sits under his awning, a slim-waisted man wearing a short, richly decorated skirt, and jeweled bracelets on his arms. The Cretan mariners, though clean-shaven, are of a different build from the Egyptians; tall and slim, with dark curling hair and long side-locks falling over one shoulder. So the vessels pass, ours going south to Thebes, the other north, to pass out into the "Great Green Sea," as the Egyptians call it, to that lonely island far out in the ocean which few Egyptians have ever seen.

We pass Buto, which was the old northern capital in ancient times, before Upper and Lower Egypt were united by Menes, the founder of the First Dynasty. Now it is just another provincial town with its temples, houses and gardens, but its ancient greatness is commemorated in one of the royal insignia which the King wears on his crown—the serpent, which was the emblem of Buto. The other royal insignia which appears beside the serpent is the falcon, the emblem of Nekhen, the old capital of southern Egypt. Although nearly fifteen hundred years separate Menes from the present King, Tuthmosis III, he still wears these two emblems to commemorate the unification of the two kingdoms, and one of his ceremonial titles is "King of Upper and Lower Egypt."

It will take us eight or nine days to reach Thebes, a long, wearisome journey. The Vizier prefers to work in the early morning and in the cool of the evening, reserving the afternoon for sleep. From time to time he dines in his cabin, sometimes takes a stroll on the deck and talks to the captain, and at the end of each day the boat moors at the quayside of some provincial town and Rekhmire and his staff sleep at the house of some local official.

But now it is early morning and we are leaving the Delta behind. The broad green plain begins to narrow, and to right and left the brown desert hills approach. From now on, for three hundred miles, we shall never lose sight of those twin deserts, the Libyan on the west and the Arabian on the east. Far away to the right, standing on the high brown plateau are the pyramids, golden against the morning blue of the sky. First, Dedefre's pyramid at Abu Roash and then the familiar trio which we know as the Giza Group—the Great Pyramid of Cheops, the pyramid of Chephren, and the small pyramid of Mycerinus. The time of which we are writing, that of Tuthmosis III, was three thousand years and more before our epoch. Yet to Rekhmire, gazing out at them from his boat, the pyramids are already ancient monuments. Cheops died nearly fifteen hundred years before Rekhmire was born, and Cheops's *Khufu* Pyramid was far from being the oldest.

As we travel farther south other pyramids appear out of the haze: Zawiyet-el-Arayan, Abusir (though they were not then known by these Arabic names, of course), and Sakkara. At Sakkara the great Step Pyramid rises proudly above its white enclosing wall, the work of Imhotep, architect of King Djoser, who reigned before Cheops, as did Snofru, whose pyramids greet the Vizier's gaze a few miles south of Sakkara. To Rekhmire and the men of his time these ancient Pharaohs of the Old Kingdom are almost creatures of legend. As a royal official, Rekhmire knows his history. He knows that, in the intervening millennium dynasties have risen and fallen, and that the capital of Egypt has shifted several times. The Old Kingdom monarchs ruled from Memphis, whose towers and temples the Vizier can see rising ahead of him, opposite Djoser's Step Pyramid. Then, after some five hundred years, at the end of the Sixth Dynasty, the power of the kings declined and there followed one hundred years of confusion, during which the central power broke up and Egypt suffered foreign invasion. Then a new, strong Dynasty arose, the Eleventh; new kings ruled the country from Hermonthis and later from Thebes. Again, after four hundred years, came collapse and the invasion of the Asiatic "Shepherd Kings." Finally, salvation had come through the warrior-kings of the Seventeenth Dynasty, who, a few hundred years before the Vizier's time, had driven out the invaders and established a stable kingdom. It was one of the successors of these kings, Tuthmosis, also a warrior, who now ruled Egypt. And Thebes, from a small provincial center, the head of a *nome*, had become the rich and powerful capital of an empire which stretched from the Sudan to the Euphrates.

Yes, the Vizier reflects as he disembarks at Memphis, Egypt has seen many changes since the Great Ones were buried in the pyramids which he can see on the far side of the river. Kings did not build pyramids nowadays; instead, they hollowed out deep, rock-cut tombs in the Theban hills. Nobles like himself no longer built stone *mastabas* [1] beside their royal master's monument. They too

---

[1] A rectangular tomb with sloping sides, so called because it recalls the shape of the *mastaba*, or stone bench, outside Arab houses.

had their rock-cut tombs in the Necropolis, not in the Royal Valley, of course, but on the other side of the mountain. Which reminds him: he must see how his own tomb is progressing, since, like all Egyptians of rank, he is preparing his own "Eternal Habitation" during his lifetime.

And yet, in other ways, the Vizier knows that much remains the same, that he has inherited a tradition handed down from those ancient kings, the founders of the Egyptian State. He worships the same gods as they did, using the same or similar rituals. The scenes which his artists were even now painting on the walls of his tomb: Rekhmire receiving his food offerings, Rekhmire supervising his farms and estates, Rekhmire entertaining his guests at a banquet, Rekhmire spearing fish in the Nile—all these can be seen in the tombs of his predecessors who had served Cheops in this town of Memphis nearly fifteen centuries ago.

Above all, the system of law and government which it was his duty to administer had been handed down, with some modifications, from those far-off rulers.

What was this tradition of government?

First, a strong centralized power, authoritarian and absolute. The achievements of Egypt during the Old, Middle, and New Kingdoms were due to the fact that the Pharaohs of that time had complete mastery of the country. Through their unchallenged control of man power they were able to carry out public works and to raise monuments which still inspire awe even in the twentieth century.

Second, a tradition of rigid bureaucratic control. Ultimate power rested with the Pharaoh, who appointed his own ministers and officials, often choosing members of the royal family. Other officials held their posts by inheritance. They were rarely elected. Under them were armies of minor officials, inspectors, tax collectors, scribes, and the like.

It is doubtful if any country in the world has been more highly administered than Ancient Egypt. While this had the bad effect of tying the country in a bureaucratic net and stultifying progress, it was to some extent inevitable. The reason was that, apart from the gold mines and the spoils of foreign conquests, the wealth of Egypt lay in its man power and its land, and the land in turn depended on the annual flooding of the Nile. It was the duty of the officials to see that this man power was organized and effectively used, that the flooding of the river, as far as possible, was accurately predicted and regulated by means of canals and irrigation works, and that the resultant wealth was channeled by taxation towards the central power.

Memphis, one of the cities which Rekhmire is visiting on his way south, was in ancient times the capital, but now it is simply the chief city of the Memphite *nome* or province. At this time, the period of the New Kingdom, there are sixty-seven of these nomes, forty-two in Upper (*i.e.,* southern) Egypt and twenty-five in Lower Egypt. The Vizier stays the night with the Governor, and the following day consults with him on matters needing his attention. They sit, with their staffs, in a columned and frescoed hall, open on one side to a garden in which fountains splash gently into ornamental pools, and birds flit among the acacias. Local officials come and go, prostrating themselves as they enter. Scribes are in attendance, sitting cross-legged on the floor and entering the Vizier's decisions on their scrolls. First there is a heated dispute about the provincial boundaries, calling for a consultation of the ancient records. Next, the delicate question of tax arrears. But then last year's crops were poor, says the Governor; a little time is needed. The Vizier is not satisfied. Is the Governor sure that the taxes were not paid? They have not been diverted into the pockets of some local official? There have been such cases of peculation before. The Governor promises to investigate.

Next the assessment for the coming year is discussed. Experts are called in to give their opinion on the next inundation. Will it be a "good Nile" or a "bad Nile"? On the judgment of the men who study the "nilometers" which register the rise of the water, will depend the estimate of the agricultural yield and the resulting tax assessment. Then there are other questions; an adequate labor force to repair dikes and canals and perhaps build new ones. The official responsible for the *corvée* (impressment of forced labor) is called in for consultation.

The morning wears on; the sun rises higher; the Vizier and his staff begin to smother yawns. They retire for their midday meal and a rest in the heat of the afternoon. The hall is empty. The drowsy sentries lean on their spears and there is no sound but the splash of the fountains and the faint sound of laughter and music from the women's quarters. Down on the water front where the crew while away the time until their masters return, the brothels and the beerhouses are full.

In the evening there are more conferences. This time the Vizier consults his "corner men," officials appointed directly by the Pharaoh and not by the Governor of the *nome.* They are District Inspectors, four from each province, and among other things they are responsible for the census lists, not only of men, but of cattle. They give their reports, but the Vizier questions them sharply. Are they sure that the lists are accurate? For Rekhmire knows only too well the habit of the *fellahin* of driving their cattle into the uplands to escape the census.

The reports of these royal representatives are useful to Rekhmire because they act as a check on the local officials, who are appointed by the provincial Governor and therefore owe their chief loyalty to the Governor, who is from a local family. He appoints the prefects who govern the cities, the scribes of the records who keep registers of lands and deeds, the chief judges, the chiefs of police and so on. Again, the *saru,* the chiefs of the country districts, are independent of the royal service; they judge suits concerning contracts, wills, and sales; they settle the *corvée* and local taxation. But the District Inspectors are independent of local control and report direct to the Vizier. Thus there are two interlocking systems: the council of landowners and their chief of the province; and the Vizier and his District Inspectors, observing affairs. Rekhmire and his royal master have constantly to watch that these local princelings do not get too powerful and independent.

But one thing all these people have in common: they all belong to the official, administering class. And as the Vizier and his staff are driven down to the quay to re-embark for their journey, they hardly glance at the brown-skinned laborers working in the hot sun, driving teams of oxen, bending their backs over the furrows, widening the irrigation canals while the foremen stand by with whips in their hands. For these laborers, the backbone of Egypt, life is an almost endless round of toil, only ending in a nameless grave on the desert fringes. They do not look up as the procession of white-robed officials drives by. Nor do they take more than a passing glance at the flotilla of ships as it moves upstream again while the Governor drives back to his lodge, thinking, "Well, that's over"—at least until the Vizier's next visit.

One by one the pyramids on the western bank glide by; Dashur, where the monuments of Snofru lean against the empty sky; Meydûm, immense and solitary; all now deserted, plundered more than one thousand years ago. The valley widens, narrows, the river turns and twists between the enclosing cliffs and then the hills step back again and leave space for more flat, green fields, with here and there a mud-brick village rising above the palm trees. And now there are no more pyramids, only deserts. Our men chant as they haul on their oars, and often the Vizier looks up from his work to watch a boat gliding past on its way north. Here is one with a huge 100-foot obelisk lying along its deck. It has come from the granite quarries of Assuan, five hundred miles to the south. The laden ship sits low in the water.[2] Here, near the marshy banks where the papyrus grows, light skiffs dart rapidly back and forth. A nobleman in a white kilt is doing a little wild-fowling. The shouts of the hunters come faintly across the waters; white geese rise in clouds, and a curved throwing stick soars among them. Two of the birds fall fluttering into the water and a boat goes out to pick them up. Once our men raise a shout and

[2] Some of these boats could carry 650 tons.

a member of the crew hurls a harpoon at a crocodile. But he misses, and amid the jeers of the sailors our flotilla moves on.

We make other calls. At Abydos the Vizier goes ashore to make an offering in the Tomb of Osiris; farther upriver he visits a town which has been raided by nomads from the western desert. There are accusations and counteraccusations between the prefect and the commander of the local garrison. Rekhmire reprimands both of them, but privately decides to recommend the appointment of another commander, and the strengthening of the garrison. So it goes on. In one place the local officials have been evading their income tax; in another there is a dispute on the payment of customs; and in yet another Rekhmire meets a deputation of pilots and steersmen, who allege nonpayment of their dues. He is very glad when, at the end of the long journey, he sees the river traffic becoming thicker, and gardens clustering along the eastern bank, and away to the right, the serrated crest of the Theban hills, which tell him that he is approaching the imperial capital, his home.

To the Vizier, his staff, and some of his crew, the first sight of Thebes is like the moment when, after a long absence, a Londoner sees London, or a Parisian approaches Paris. It is the seat of his government, the focus of his patriotic emotion, his workshop, his playground, his home. Also, in the case of the Egyptian, it is something even more important, the burial place of his ancestors. And this double function, a home for the living and a resting place for the dead, is emphasized by the fact that the city is really two towns, divided by the river. On our right as our ship approaches the quays is a ridge of brown hills, cracked and fissured and baked by the sun. They rise abruptly from the flat river plain, and below them, with their backs to the cliffs, is a string of magnificent stone buildings. These are the funerary temples of the kings, who are now beginning to be buried in a lonely valley on the far side of the hills. In those hills is the vast Necropolis. The cliffs, and the low ground in front of them, are honeycombed with rock-cut tombs of nobles and the richer Thebans.[3] Between the cliffs and the river are large villages of mud-brick houses, populated entirely by those whose work lies in the Necropolis. Here live the embalmers, the makers of coffins and funerary furniture, the quarrymen who hollow out the tombs, and the artists and sculptors who adorn their walls. Near the temples live the priests whose duty it is to make the regular food offerings for the spirits of the dead. All, in some way or other, serve the vast, silent population whose bodies lie hidden in their dark chambers within the hills.

But turn your eyes to the left and you see a complete contrast, the city of the living—a rich, swarming, noisy city, crowded with life. Small craft dart in and out among the hundreds of ships moored at the quaysides—ships with high, curving prows and tall masts; merchant vessels unloading grain and other produce; barges freighted with stone blocks for the temples and palaces; foreign ships from Syria and from the Aegean islands; warships, and the richly gilded craft of the Pharaoh and his nobles. A dull, confused murmur floats across the water as our flotilla approaches the quayside and the sailors stand with ropes in their hands preparing to make fast. And as we look beyond

[3] Thebes is, of course, a Greek name. In the time of which we are writing the city was called No-Amun.

the water front, we see a huddle of mud-brick walls which are warehouses, stores, customhouses, shops, beerhouses, brothels, and the dwellings of the poor. Beyond them, fenced in by high walls enclosing gardens, are the houses of the nobles and the richer officials; but these too are of mud-brick and timber, and from the outside are imposing only because of their size. The only stone building of any consequence is the great Temple of Amun-Re, King of the Gods, the pylons and obelisks of which had been visible on our left as we approached the city.

And now we are alongside. The Vizier's servants and guards are waiting for him at the quayside. Men in white kilts and carrying staffs clear a way for him through the crowd; the nearest members touch their foreheads in the dust as he passes. He mounts his gilded chariot, and then, preceded by runners, drives through the streets to his mansion in the suburbs. Rekhmire has come home.

# CHAPTER 3

# HOUSES AND FURNITURE

**H**AVING tried to give the reader an impression of Egypt as it would be seen by a high official of the Eighteenth Dynasty, I am going to make a short digression into earlier Egyptian history. It is tempting immediately to follow Rekhmire into his Theban home, and to meet his wife and children. However, that would limit us too strictly to one particular period of Egyptian history, and the subject of this chapter—houses and furniture—calls for a much wider sweep. In addition we shall be in a better position to understand Rekhmire's social and domestic background if we know something of the two thousand years of developing civilization which lay behind it. So for the time being let us leave the Vizier to his homecoming; we shall return to him in the next chapter.

A settled home, a permanent dwelling with its furniture and equipment, is necessary for the development of certain arts and sciences. Not all of them, of course. In poetry, philosophy, and mathematics, the nomadic Arabs reached heights which the Egyptians never attained. But even the Arabs were unable to achieve their miracles of architecture and design until they established cities. Although the Ancient Egyptians were among the first—perhaps were the first—people to develop the art of writing and produce a literature, they were a long-settled people whose greatest triumphs were in architecture, sculpture, and painting. Also, because they were a settled people, they early developed the art of government and civil administration.

Climate and available building materials decide the form of a people's buildings. In northern Europe with its harsh winters and great forests, timber was the first building material to be used when men moved down into the lowlands from their rough stone huts on the treeless moors. But as soon as they had learned the art of working stone, they began to build in this material or in brick; durability and protection from wind, rain, snow, and ice were and are essential. In Egypt these conditions obviously do not apply. The country enjoys almost perpetual sunshine, and during many months of the year the climate is uncomfortably hot, especially in the south. The main need was for shelter from the sun and the cold night air. Stone existed in abundance, but even after the Egyptians had settled in the Nile Valley they rarely used stone for domestic buildings. They used instead that which remains to this day the cheapest, most accessible and most easily workable building material in Egypt—*mud*.

To people living in more temperate climates mud would seem a messy, impermanent, unsatisfactory medium. Not so in Egypt. At Sakkara, and near the Great Pyramid at Giza, I have seen *mastaba* tombs built of dried mud-brick which have survived for more than five thousand years. Earlier in this book I have stated that the reason for the disappearance of Ancient Egyptian towns was the perishable nature of the building material. This, however, was due only to the fact that it is easy to destroy. The

Egyptians had no reason to preserve their old homes, so when they wanted new ones, they simply pulled them down and built again. With their tombs it was different, and the chief damage to these was done by the tomb robbers.

When the Nile recedes, it leaves acres of brown mud which rapidly turns to grey under the sun. As it dries, it splits, and in the early days of Egyptian civilization the people probably built their dwellings from these naturally formed blocks, the way some of the *fellahin* do today. Later they learned to make blocks by mixing the mud with water. Often the blocks were strengthened by mixing in straw and cattle dung. To this day the *fellahin* live in a village of mud and dung, which have a strange unfinished appearance. There is, of course, no need for a sloping roof to drain off the rain, so the roofs are left flat, usually with the unfinished walls projecting irregularly above to allow for the addition of another story if necessary. The flat roofs are pleasant to sit on in the cool of the evening, and in Old Cairo, where ground space is restricted, many people keep their animals up there. It is quite common, when walking through the Old City, to look up and meet the reflective gaze of a cow.

The villages and towns of Ancient Egypt were very like this, as we know from the numerous examples of model mud-brick houses, called "soul houses" which the Ancient Egyptians left in their tombs. There are illustrations on Plates 11 and 12.

There were other building materials: timber (though at first this was sparingly used as there are no big timber trees in Egypt), palm ribs, reeds, and the stalks of the papyrus plant which then grew plentifully along the river-banks. Petrie, whose *Social Life in Ancient Egypt* is one of the most useful sources of information, believes that in pre-Dynastic times (before 3200 B.C.) the early chiefs had portable timber houses which, during the inundation could be moved up to the desert in a day, and in spring, when the pastures were green, could be moved down among the reed huts of the shepherds.

The planks, about 12 to 14 inches wide, and 6 to 7 feet high, were set upright, overlapping so as to form a panel-pattern. Being lashed together at the edges, the overlap was kept close, and slid to and fro, as the night dews or sirocco expanded or contracted the wood. The doorways were all along the sides, so as to give plenty of air when still and warm. They projected into the hall, and so left sleeping places between each, where the chief's followers could sleep as a guard around the hall. This pattern of house gave rise to the copying of external panelling *in brick work* [our italics] for the "eternal house" of the dead chief, a pattern which lasted down to the Eighteenth Dynasty.

The palm ribs, or reeds, lashed together in bundles and bound with mud, were used as pillars before these were made of wood or stone. Even today one can see such pillars supporting the heavy *shaduf* or water hoist which the *fellah* uses to raise water from a lower to a higher canal. But the most interesting point is that when, round about 2800 B.C., the Egyptians began to build monumentally in stone, they imitated these earlier forms. Thus at Sakkara, near the Step

Pyramid of Djoser, one can see fluted columns, which an-
ticipate the Doric column by more than two thousand
years, the form of which may have been derived from the
bundles of reeds which originally supported the roofs of
mud-brick houses. Another use of reeds, and palm ribs, was
to mix them with mud and lay them across the timber
rafters of a house as roofing. This method is still in use
throughout Egypt. Logs of wood were used in pre-Dynastic
times as door lintels, and you can still see the cylindrical
form imitated in stone above the "false doors" of the later
stone *mastabas*.

Another feature of all except the very poorest Egyptian houses, in ancient times and today, is the courtyard.
In a country such as Egypt, with its almost perpetual sunshine, the courtyard is the natural place for daily life. So
in nearly all these model houses you will notice a walled
court in front of the house, or in the case of larger houses,
there is a courtyard with rooms opening off it on all four
sides. Often there is a stone tank for water in the center of
the court. One can see a similar arrangement in the Roman
villas of Pompeii; there, as in Egypt, the household looked
inwards, not outwards.

The Egyptian houses presented a forbidding exterior:
blank mud-brick walls pierced, high up, by very small
windows. So fierce is the Egyptian sunlight that only small
apertures are necessary to illuminate the interior. Inside the
house the rooms facing the inner courtyard often had no
windows but were usually open on the side facing the
court; the reflected sunlight was sufficient to light the interior. There were also broad loggias, supported on pillars,
overlooking cool, shady gardens, all surrounded by high

walls which shut them from the outside world. It was the exact opposite of life in northern Europe, where the windows look outwards onto the street. In Egypt they looked inwards.

Gradually, over the centuries, certain features of Egyptian houses changed. The homes of the nobles became larger and more luxurious; pillars of stone or timber replaced those of palm ribs, and the mud-brick walls were coated with fine plaster and adorned with colored frescoes. But it is doubtful if the houses of the very poor altered very much.

With certain exceptions there was little attempt at town planning. Great cities like Memphis and Thebes simply grew haphazardly, like medieval London. Even in Akhnaten's "new" city at Tell-el-Amarna, although the main thoroughfares are laid out in a roughly rectilinear pattern, the suburbs straggle off in a bewildering tangle of lanes and alleys. The only exceptions occurred when the Pharaoh ordered some big public work and a town was specially created to house the workmen. I have seen one such city at Medinet Habu. It is like a barracks: straight, narrow streets built at right angles, and hundreds of small, rectangular houses of practically identical pattern. Petrie describes another of these towns, at Kahun, built in the Twelfth Dynasty.

The houses may be of any size, from four rooms to six, and each street contains a uniform size of house. The streets vary in length; one is 62 feet long for two houses; others are 230 feet long for eight or nine houses. . . . The streets vary from 11 to 15 feet wide.

They had a channel down the middle for a drain, like the old English kennel. There was no separate footway, because there were no vehicles in such a town.

The simple houses had an open court opposite to the entrance, a common room on one side, and the store rooms on the other, with a stairway up to the roof. The larger type for artisans had an open court, four rooms opening off it, and five others dependent on the outer rooms. . . . The fire was usually against one side of a room, with a few bricks to support the cooking pots. The doors were of wood, with wooden sills and a lintel built into the wall; when the pivot holes were worn down a bit of leather was put under the pivot, usually a bit of worn-out sandal. . . .

Allowing for the difference of climate and custom, such artisans' houses were probably superior to the "back-to-back" workers' dwellings in Britain's industrial North.

Sanitation and drainage, as we understand them, were never developed as they were by some other ancient cultures—for example, by the Minoans of Crete. At Knossos the great Palace of Minos, parts of which were built two thousand years before Christ, had an elaborate and scientific system of drainage. Rain water was carried from the roof through pipes let into the walls, and thence into underground sewers big enough to accommodate a stooping man. Waste water from bathrooms was led away to these pipes, and in the Queen's Megaron there survives to this day a primitive toilet which, Sir Arthur Evans believed, had a system for flushing the basin. The Ancient Egyptians did not have such an elaborate system for the simple reason that they did not need it. Roofs were drained in order to prevent water collecting and causing leaks, but, unlike Crete, Egypt has so little rainfall that underground street drainage was unnecessary.

The disposal of refuse and human excrement was another matter. In the poorer parts of the towns refuse was probably left lying about to be devoured by scavenger dogs and birds, as it still is in many Egyptian towns today. My reason for believing this is that in the ancient medical papyri which have come down to us, a high proportion of the cases with which the Ancient Egyptian doctors had to deal were eye diseases, which are still the scourge of Egypt. These diseases, trachoma and ophthalmia, are carried by the flies which breed among refuse. Incidentally, the other prevalent Egyptian disease, bilharzia or schistosomiasis, also occurred in Ancient Egypt. It is caused by a small worm which gets into the blood stream and causes obstruction in the liver, heart or lungs; the disease is propagated by the *fellah's* insanitary habit of defecating and urinating in or near the canals and irrigation ditches. Tiny organisms from the stools or urine of an infected person enter into the bodies of certain species of snails, where they breed and produce other organisms which penetrate human skin and enter the blood stream, where they develop into the bilharzia worm. Specimens of these worms have been found in Ancient Egyptian mummies.

However, before we condemn the poor Egyptian peasant for his insanitary habits, we should bear in mind his working conditions. For most of his day he worked on the land, which meant that he was always in or near water, for the fertility of the soil depended on a network of canals and ditches. Even if the *fellahin* had latrines in their homes they were only there at night. During the day they had no choice.

Earth closets have been found in the ruins of large and small Egyptian houses, though it does not seem to be known whether these were connected to an underground cesspit, or cleared daily. Personally, I suspect that the cesspit method was known. At several villages in Lower Egypt, Egyptian and European doctors, who are trying to improve sanitary conditions, showed me the *fellahin's* own system of dealing with human refuse, which is certainly very ancient. These villagers dig a deep pit and line it with hard-baked brick which is impervious to water, and over it the latrine is built. At the end of several months they open the pit, clean out the refuse, leave it to the sun for a period in order to kill the poisons, and then spread it on their land as a fertilizer. This method may have been used in Pharaonic times.

The palaces of the kings and the mansions of the great were, of course, far more beautiful and luxurious than the homes of lesser men, and by the Eighteenth Dynasty, when Rekhmire lived, they had reached a pitch of comfort and refinement which could hardly be improved even in the present day. In fact, I suspect that in some respects they were probably more comfortable, and certainly far better adapted to the climate, than the blocks of European-type flats which the rich modern Egyptian inhabits on the outskirts of Cairo.

They were still built of mud-brick blocks, but the walls were adorned with delicate frescoes of trees and plants and birds in gay colors. Some delightful examples of these were discovered by Sir Flinders Petrie at Tell-el-Amarna, and they can be seen in the Ashmolean Museum at Oxford. In size and plan these houses varied according to the wealth and status of the owner, but certain basic features remained constant. First, there was a high outer wall, enclosing a garden. This wall was pierced by one sole entrance, which admitted the visitor to the porter's lodge. If it was a very large house, there would be three passages from this lodge: one to the best rooms of the house with columned halls for reception, and smaller rooms for dining and sleeping; the second led to the women's quarters, which were separate from those of the men; here lived the lord's harem; the third passage led to the servants' quarters, with its dining hall, kitchens, and storerooms. The family rooms comprised about sixteen rooms with three halls of columns; the women's quarters contained twelve rooms or more with perhaps one hall of columns, while the kitchen and stores comprised about fourteen rooms with a servants' hall. Right at the back of the house would be a large open court with a shady colonnade, and perhaps more storerooms. There would thus be a total of about fifty to sixty rooms, all approached by one narrow entrance for protection. This is the kind of house in which lived very high officials like Rekhmire.

There was also a somewhat smaller type of house used by the middle-class officials. These houses were about 50 feet square surrounded by a garden wall, pierced as usual by one door leading to the porter's lodge. From there you would walk along an open loggia on the north side of the house, to reach the central hall of columns. From this four groups of rooms opened: the master's room with its bed;

the women's quarters and the kitchen; the men's quarters, sometimes with a secondary hall; and a group of small store-rooms. From here stairs led up to the roof. The floors of these rooms were usually paved, and if the ground was damp the Egyptians had an ingenious system of sinking short cylinders, like drainpipes, vertically in the ground, and laying a brick paving on top of them.

It will be seen that the household of an Egyptian official of high rank was a large one. Not only were there rooms for himself, his guests and his servants, but also for his grown-up children, if they were unmarried, and for the children of his several wives. There would also be accommodation for his chariots and horses, storerooms for food, cellars for wine, and conical granaries for grain. These were sometimes in the garden, but in small houses they were built on the roof. The picture on Plate 9 will help to explain the layout of one of these large houses.

But it should always be remembered that most of the life of the Ancient Egyptians was lived out of doors, as is life in southern Europe today. Rooms were only used at night and during the winter months. It would be in the courts and gardens that we would find the Egyptian official taking his relaxation. They were great garden lovers, perhaps out of defiance towards the grim, sterile deserts which hemmed them in. Trees were brought from Asia to supplement the few indigenous Egyptian species, carefully planted and tenderly nurtured. There were trees for fruit and trees for shade, but the bright light would penetrate the leaves, allowing for the free growth of plants and flowers underneath. There were also big ornamental tanks for fish.

57

A great gardener could rise to high rank. One of the most charming tombs in the Theban Necropolis is that of Senufer, Head Gardener to the King. The rough rock ceiling is left in its natural state, and painted to represent vine trellises, so that one appears to be walking under clusters of hanging grapes. Only a man of importance would be allowed to make a tomb in the Necropolis, or indeed could afford one.

The furniture of Egyptian homes varied with the importance of the owner, but, generally speaking, there was less of it than in European or American houses. However, in the homes of the kings and the nobles such furniture as did exist was beautiful to look at and finely made. The principal articles were beds, chairs, tables, and chests for clothes and other articles. Lovely examples of these have been preserved in Egyptian tombs, mainly of the Eighteenth and Nineteenth Dynasties, and other examples are depicted on the wall reliefs and paintings.

To take the chairs first; there would be fewer of these than in a European house of comparable size, because the Egyptians had the Oriental habit of sitting or half kneeling on the floor or on cushioned divans. Guests at parties are often shown in this posture, with their knees tucked under them (see illustration on Plate 14). They never seem to have adopted a reclining position when dining, as did the Greeks and Romans.

Nor did they sit around a communal dining table. The tables depicted in tomb paintings were small affairs and at a party each guest would have his own table, set with delicacies which were served to him by a slave.

Describing the construction of this furniture, Petrie writes:

> The design of Egyptian furniture is always excellent, mechanically. The joints have angle pieces of naturally-bent grain. The chair backs are well supported with diagonal struts behind, like old Windsor chairs. The tall thin legs of tables are held in by a crossbar and diagonal struts. The lines of couches and chairs are flowing and harmonious, the proportions look safe and true, without being clumsy. A most ingenious form of spring served for suspending the portable shrines; straight at one end and curved at the other, the weight, which was hung near each end, contracted the straight length and expanded the curve, so that the total length, framed in, remained equal.

Personally, I find some Eighteenth Dynasty furniture overornate. The famous Throne of Tutankhamun is to my mind clumsy and overloaded with ornament. I prefer the charming child's chair (Plate 10) of wood inlaid with ivory, which was also found in the tomb and was presumably used by the King when he was a small boy. Even more vulgar were some of the palace ornaments found in Tutankhamun's tomb. Take the well-known boat-shaped shrine of alabaster. It is beautifully made, and the material is lovely, but apart from the charming little figure of Queen Ankhesnamun with her fan (she sits in the prow of the boat), the article seems to me not much better than certain specimens of Victoriana.

Hardly any furniture has come down to us from the Old Kingdom, but the few examples which have survived, with representations on wall reliefs, indicate that the standard of design was far higher in the time of the Pyramid-builders. Some of the simplicity, strength, and majesty which one sees in the diorite statue of Chaephren seems to have entered into the design of such furniture. The most superb examples are, of course, the bed, chair, canopy, and carrying-chair of Queen Hetephras, the mother of Cheops, which were found, with her empty sarcophagus, in a deep shaft near the Great Pyramid.

Ancient Egyptian beds are interesting. They are built much higher off the ground than the beds of today, and sometimes the mattress sloped slightly from head to foot. The bedframes were formed from massive poles tapering at the ends. The miter jointing was quite varied; six different types of joint have been identified. The mattress itself was of cord matting, stretched tightly, but having a certain resilience. They were presumably covered with cushions, and people who have slept on them say they are quite comfortable. Petrie even alleged that the wooden headrest was comfortable, but this I find hard to believe.

These semicircular headrests have always been something of a puzzle to modern minds, but they are still in use today in certain parts of Africa. They are shaped to fit under the neck, near the ears, presumably in order to keep the heavy wigs which the Egyptians wore clear of the bed. But it is difficult to see why they did not take their wigs off at night. Perhaps they only used these rests when relaxing during the day.

Petrie also alleged, on what grounds I cannot discover,

that the Ancient Egyptians slept in a "straight-out" position, whereas most of us today curl up. He points out that the bodies of the pre-Dynastic Egyptians were buried in a crouching position, knees under the chin, whereas during Dynastic times they were buried, lying straight. But burial customs are no indication of sleeping habits.

It must not be thought that all Egyptian furniture was well made. The Egyptians were as familiar as we are with the jerry-builder and the maker of gimcrack furniture. Sometimes he would fake a mortise-and-tenon joint, allowing the tenon to penetrate only a short distance into the wood and then clapping on a piece of inlay on the other side to make it appear that the joint went right through. Cheap wood was covered with veneer; ivory inlays were imitated with white paint. As for "graining" with paint, there was no trick used by the Victorian faker which the Egyptians did not know. They imitated grain-wood patterning, with all the characteristic knots and undulations, as far back as the Third Dynasty (2800 B.C.); they even imitated valuable stone vases in wood. Granite was faithfully copied in paint, and at Amarna, limestone columns were found painted to represent glazed tiles. Even inlaid jewelry was imitated with colored glazes.

If the Egyptians of the New Empire had shared our passion for antiquity, no doubt they would have produced "genuine antiques" of the Old Kingdom to sell to collectors. Fortunately for archaeologists they did not, which is just as well; the skillful fakes of their modern descendants are quite difficult enough to deal with.

Other articles of furniture in Egyptian homes were chests for linen, clothes, and other articles. These were often beautifully made and inlaid with ivory, lapis lazuli, carnelian, and other materials. The finest examples are those found in the tomb of Tutankhamun. Lighting was by oil lamps, and some of these were of thin translucent alabaster, painted on the inside with a colored design which showed through when a wick was lit inside the lamp. There were also miniature shrines containing figures of Amun, Isis, Osiris, and other gods. In the houses of the king and his wealthier subjects, gold and silver were frequently used in furniture and ornaments. An Egyptian feast, with the soft light gleaming on the gold and silver of the furniture, bringing out the glow of red carnelian and deep blue lapis lazuli, must have been a beautiful sight, especially when one adds to it the glitter of bracelets and necklaces and the jewels of the women.

But what did they eat? Among the wealthier classes the diet seems to have been rich and varied. In tomb paintings of feasts we see fowl, probably boiled, grilled or roasted; and beef was also eaten, either roasted or grilled. In their prayers for the deceased the Egyptians asked that his nourishment in Heaven should be bread and beer, beef and goose. Ten different sorts of meat are mentioned, five kinds of birds, and eleven varieties of fruit, "and all manner of sweet things." Fashion entered a lot into eating, the favorite dishes varying from age to age—again among the rich. Erman points out in his *Life in Ancient Egypt* that a Nineteenth Dynasty king had set down in an inscription the meals he ate on a journey through various towns with his court, and "in the list of ten varieties of bread and five sorts of cake there is scarcely one which was in common use under the Old Empire."

Like us, they occasionally liked to try foreign dishes, and in one sacred book it is stated that the gods "eat the fine bread of *Quamh*"—a Semitic speciality. The Egyptian people also knew of and obtained good wine from Charu, beer from Quede, fine oil from "Ersa, Cheta, Sangar, and T'echesa"—all foreign towns.

As to the preparation of food, not much is known. Goose, the favorite national dish, was roasted over live embers. Fish was roasted in the same way.

Breadmaking was always very important. Probably the Egyptians had no mills. They pounded the corn with great pestles. Finer flour was obtained by rubbing the corn between two stones. Then they kneaded the dough (usually the women performed this task and there are many models showing the process) and then the round flat cakes were lightly baked over the coals. Some of the shapes in which the cakes were made are remarkably like modern pastries. But I suspect that they tasted very like Arab bread today—like tough cardboard.

Beer and wine were the staple drinks. Beer was the favorite drink of the Egyptian people and there are many models from Twelfth Dynasty towns showing the brewing process. Beer was made from ground barley, or, as it was called, "the corn of Upper Egypt." Under the Old Kingdom there were four kinds, including "black beer" and "beer of a dark color."

Wine was drunk by the kings and nobles, and in the Palace of Akhnaten, excavated at Tell-el-Amarna by Petrie and others, wine jars have been found inscribed with the vintage. Judging from some of the poems and tomb inscriptions, drunkenness was common, in fact encouraged. But although the results of excess are vividly depicted, there is no record of a hangover cure!

When eating, the Ancient Egyptians of the Old Kingdom squatted on the ground, though in Rekhmire's time chairs and stools were used by people of importance. They ate with their fingers, and after eating, water was poured over the hands as in the Orient today. One sees depicted in the dining rooms of the great, jugs and basins almost exactly like a Victorian washstand. The tables were decked with flowers, and the guests wore flowers in their hair. The love of flowers and green plants was always a characteristic of the Ancient Egyptian people.

And now, having learned something of their houses, their furniture and domestic habits, let us meet the people themselves.

# CHAPTER 4

# THE VIZIER GIVES A PARTY

HAVING rested after his long journey and made his report to Pharaoh, Rekhmire has decided to celebrate his home-coming with a party, to which we are invited.

Across the river, the sun is setting behind the Theban hills, and in the great Temple of Amun-Re the priests are chanting their last offices, their hands outstretched to Re as he goes to "his Horizon." After the stupefying heat of the day, a refreshing coolness begins to descend upon Thebes, reviving and stimulating the city. Down by the quaysides the boatmen shout to each other; music and hand clapping float out from the beer shops and eating houses along the water front; a woman leans out of an upper window and calls to a passing sailor, whose rude reply provokes a stream of answering abuse.

Petitioners who have waited vainly all afternoon at the gateway of some great official get wearily to their feet, wrap their cloaks around them and pad their way home along the narrow streets, their bare feet kicking up little puffs of grey dust.

We will assume we are Theban residents living a little distance from the Vizier's house. At the appointed time the chariot is brought round by our servants. We mount and, accompanied by two or three runners with torches, begin our brief drive. The streets are crowded. Often we have to pull to the side of the narrow road to allow a string of cattle to pass. Once, at a crossroad, we are held up for five minutes while a detachment of soldiers marches past, the bare-chested men carrying spears and shields, their officers marching ahead of them. Then the streets begin to widen; we drive past high walls over which palm trees peep, and the porters sit outside their lodges on three-legged stools, enjoying the evening air and chatting with their friends. Once a dog rushes out of an alleyway, snapping at our horses' heels until driven off by the driver. The air is warm and soft, so that we need only our lightest clothes, though the servants have brought wraps for the return journey.

Now we have arrived. Our chariot draws up beside the great wall of the Vizier's house. The porter, in his best clothes and carrying his staff of office, stands by the lighted doorway directing the servants. Some come forward to direct our driver where to put the chariot. As we alight and mount the steps, other chariots are arriving with guests, slim men and elegant women in spotless robes of fluted linen, and wearing heavy black curled wigs which frame their faces. There is much laughter and conversation as, friends greet each other. And now, preceded and followed by male and female slaves, we are passing through the long corridor beside the house. It leads to the main reception room, the hall of columns.

As we enter, we are met by more slaves and hand-maidens; the men wearing the short white kilt, starched and projecting in front; the girls wearing practically nothing except wisps of fabric round the loins, and necklaces, bracelets, and anklets of colored beads. They flit in and out among the white-robed guests, presenting to each a lotus flower, and handing round small dainties and cups of wine or beer. This, of course, is before the main meal, which will be served when the visitors are seated.

Now we are in the lofty hall of columns, which are painted a dark red and have capitals shaped like lotus buds. The soft light from the alabaster lamps shines on the colored frescoes which adorn the walls—trees with birds of plumage flitting among the branches, flowers and butterflies delicately drawn on the smooth plaster. The eye travels up the columns, past the colored capitals, to the rafters of the ceiling, which are also gaily patterned. There is a babel of conversation as we edge our way through the throng of bare-shouldered women and dark, heavily wigged men to the place where the Vizier waits to greet us at the far end of the hall.

Rekhmire is a noble figure in his stiffly starched robe of fine linen, pleated in many folds, and held in by a richly ornamented girdle. His shrewd, humorous eyes smile at us and as he stretches out his hand to greet us, gold bracelets gleam on his arms. Beside him stands the lady Meryet, his Chief Wife, who, like all Egyptian women of rank, shares many of her husband's activities. She also is of noble birth and, as Tiyi—the uncharitable wife of the Chief Secretary—will tell you, Rekhmire did very well by marrying her, as her fortune was larger than his. The high status which Egyptian women enjoy is due in part to the fact that inheritance is always through the female line. Even the Pharaoh himself could only be King by marrying the royal heiress.

Meryet is a handsome woman. She is about thirty-five, twenty years younger than her husband, and though she is no longer as slim as her daughters, her figure is still good, set off by the clinging robe of almost transparent linen which frankly reveals the outlines of her body. She too wears the large wig of natural hair, curled in hundreds of tight plaits, which hangs almost to her bare shoulders. There are gold bracelets on her rounded arms, her finger- and toenails are dyed with henna, and her dark eyes are made to appear even larger and more elongated by the green-blue eye paint she has applied to them. She has spent the better part of the afternoon on her toilette and is a credit to her handmaidens.

Near her stand the two loveliest of her daughters, similarly dressed. The eldest is Nofret, tall, slim, and rather imperious. (She is a priestess of Amun, entitled to shake the *systrum* before Pharaoh as he enters the Temple to offer sacrifice. The *systrum* is a loop of metal attached to a wooden handle, with small squares of metal threaded loosely on rods fixed inside the loop. Shaken in unison, these instruments give out a not-unpleasant, jangling sound.) Nofret is rather a trial to her mother and the despair of several young men who have hopes of marrying her.

Her younger sister, Ta-kha'et, though she has not the cold, classical beauty of Nofret, makes up for it by her animation and intelligence. She is seventeen, a little shorter than her sister, and is enjoying herself. Part of her joy arises from the fact that, unlike many of her father's parties, this one, at her request, is not only for the elderly Court officials, but for their sons and daughters. Not that the daughters interest Ta-kha'et very much. She has met them all before, often. But she rarely has the opportunity

68

of meeting the young men, in one of whom, Sinuhe, the son of the Chief Secretary, she has more than a passing interest. Tiyi, Sinuhe's mother, thinks Ta-kha'et is a minx. So does Sinuhe, but in a different way.

Here is Tiyi approaching now, a thin, tight-lipped woman with the darting eyes of a bird. Meryet greets her with insincere but well-simulated cordiality; Tiyi has always been one of her trials. She knew, of course, that Rekhmire had to invite the Chief Secretary, who is one of the highest officials at court, but oh, his wife. . . . Tiyi passes on into the crowd to take her seat, and Meryet, after remarking quietly to her husband, "Where on *earth* did she get those earrings?" reassumes her smile for the next guest.

Standing beside the Vizier himself is his youngest adult son, a handsome, eighteen-year-old lad named Kenamun. Rekhmire's eldest sons, Menkheperre-Sonb and Amenhotep, are married. They and their wives are among the guests. Kenamun is an officer in the troop of picked soldiers who form the Palace Guard, known as the "Followers of His Majesty"—a post he obtained through his father's influence. But he is a restless, ambitious young man, already tiring of ceremonial duties and anxious for a little action. As he dutifully smiles and greets his father's guests, his eyes are searching the crowd for the one man he wishes to see, whom Rekhmire has said will be present. This is General Amenemhab, hero of several foreign campaigns and much admired by the young soldier. Kenamun is secretly hoping that, if the General likes him, he might persuade his father —and, even more important, his mother—to let him be transferred to foreign service. Ah, there is the General coming in now, a man of forty-five, with powerful, suntanned face and an erect, muscular figure. He smiles at Rekhmire across the room and Kenamun gives his father a curious, hopeful glance.

Other notable guests come forward, make their greetings, and move on to the room where the banquet has been prepared: the Mayor of Thebes and his wife and son; the Fanbearer to the King,[1] and his wife; the Chief Priest of Amun, and his wife and daughter; the Keeper of the Royal Garden, and his fat, homely spouse; the Royal Tutor; and the Chief Scribe and his melancholy-looking son, who is an officer of chariotry. His name is Senmut; he is a highborn but rather shy youth believed to be in love with Nofret.

So, gradually, they move out of the Hall of Reception to another columned room, where gold and inlaid chairs are arranged, in order of precedence, for the more distinguished guests. The others seat themselves on the straw mats and cushions spread around the floor, the women gracefully arranging their narrow skirts and adjusting their curled wigs. (For the manner of sitting, see the illustration of a banquet on Plate 15.) The girl slaves hang garlands of flowers round the necks of the guests, and hand to each a cake of scented grease which he or she places on top of his or her wig. During the course of the evening this will gradually melt and anoint the face and neck, which apparently gives great pleasure.

Now the feast begins. Around the room are many small tables on which the food is set—roast beef, chicken, duck, pigeon, vegetables, and a large variety of bread cut

---

[1] The bearer of this strange-sounding title was one of the most important officers in the realm, a kind of Grand Chamberlain. The office sounds servile, but compare the modern "Gentleman of the Bedchamber" and the "Mistress of the Robes."

into different shapes. Nearby stand the wine jars set in metal stands, each jar marked with the vintage year. Rekhmire is noted for his fine cellar, and as the bronze wine cups are rapidly filled and refilled, the conversation becomes more animated. Meanwhile the slaves, male and female, serve the guests with delicacies which are eaten with the hand, knives only being used to cut the meat. Little Nebet, the eight-year-old daughter of Meryet, who sits beside her mother's chair, is manfully tackling a small chicken, while her elder brother Per-hor, aged ten, is gnawing a grilled chop. Napkins and finger bowls are handed round so that the guests can deal with the grease on their hands as the steward of the household energetically directs the servants.[2]

The guests are beginning to split up into conversational groups. Rekhmire is talking to General Amenemhab about his recent trip. Young Kenamun sits beside his father, listening to every word.

"I talked to Merire at Asiut," says the Vizier. "They've had trouble with the Libyans again; the third raid in twelve months."

"I heard about it, of course," replies the General.

[2] Although social life was much freer among the Ancient Egyptians than it is among the Arabs, unmarried men and women were not allowed to mix as freely as they do in the West today. In noble houses the women lived in their own quarters, but on occasions like this both sexes could be present, as we know from many tomb paintings of the period. At the same time it seems probable that only the married couples sat together; unchaperoned meetings between young people of opposite sexes would be frowned upon, as they are in Oriental and some Western countries to this day. Nevertheless, from what we know of human nature, it is not unlikely that these barriers were occasionally crossed; for the purpose of this episode I am going to assume that they were.

I am also well aware that Oriental marriages are usually "arranged" on a basis of family alliances and property, but if I am asked to believe that young people in Ancient Egypt never fell in love, I can only express my polite disbelief.

"They caught the garrison napping. Fifty men killed in their beds before they could reach their arms. By the time the alarm was given, the raiders were away, with half the women and most of the stores."

Amenemhab frowns and looks at his ring. "I know," he says. "Merire sent me a full report, and I've had another from the garrison commander."

"Pewero?" The Vizier raises his eyebrows. "What do you think of him?"

"Not much."

"Neither does the Governor."

"I'd have had him transferred months ago, but the man I had in mind as a replacement was away in Nubia. Anyway, you'll be pleased to hear that Pewero's being recalled. The new man will leave tomorrow."

"Good."

A little distance away Meryet is talking to the wife of the Royal Tutor, who is fingering her hostess's necklace.

"It's lovely, dear," says the Tutor's wife. "Syrian?"

"Yes; my husband brought it back from Gebal—and this," she adds, holding out her arm on which a bracelet glitters. "Those are from Gebal, too," she says, nodding towards a group of fine vases which stand on a nearby table. "Oh, and some wonderful Tyrian dyed cloth—bales of it!"

"I wish my husband could travel," sighs the Tutor's wife.

"Oh, I don't know," replies Meryet, taking another slice of chicken. "Rekhmire's always away for so long; one misses him—and then the boys tend to get out of hand when their father's away."

"Per-hor looks very well, anyway," remarks her

friend, nodding towards Meryet's small son, who is showing the General a model soldier which Rekhmire has
brought back from his travels. His small sister, Nebet, not
to be outdone, runs forward dragging a toy horse on
wheels (see illustration on Plate 29). Meryet gently pulls
the child towards her, wipes Nebet's greasy little mouth,
and beckons to a stout woman slave. "They're getting un-
ruly," she says. "Take Nebet to bed and tell Per-hor that
he must go, too."

Reluctantly the two children allow themselves to be
dragged away by the stout nurse, one on each arm; the
guests wave to them as they leave the room.

Meryet holds out her cup to be refilled, and resumes
the interrupted conversation.

"It's not Per-hor who worries me," she says. "I can
cope with him. It's Kenamun. He thinks of nothing but the
Army. I thought he would be satisfied when my husband
got him into the Royal Bodyguard, but he's not. He wants
to go campaigning, like Senmut over there. You see? Kenamun's got him in a corner; talking about the Syrian campaign, I'll be bound."

For Kenamun, tiring of the conversation between his
father and the General, has found his way to the melancholy young man, Senmut, an officer of charioteers, who
has served in Pharaoh's Syrian campaigns. Senmut, who is
watching Nofret on the far side of the room, has only half
an ear for Kenamun's eager questions.

"But how high are the mountains?"

"Enormous."

"Higher than the Theban hills?"

Senmut laughs. "You could put twenty of the Theban

73

hills on top of each other and still they'd be lower than the Syrian mountains. And they're cold—by Horus, they're cold." Senmut shivers in recollection. "That's why the Syrians wear such heavy clothes." He smiles again. "Perhaps that's why they wear beards—to keep their faces warm."

Kenamun laughs too, but he is puzzled. Like most Egyptians, he has never seen a mountain, never known any climate but the warm, flat valley of the Nile.

"And there is a Nile in the sky?" he inquires.

"That's what the priests say. The water comes from the sky, it's true, but it isn't a river. It's rain."

"But we have rain here sometimes," objects Kenamun.

"You call *that* rain," laughs his companion. "Here you get only a sprinkle, which dries in an hour. There you get storms, torrents which last for days and weeks. And snow."

"Snow? What's that?"

"We haven't even a word for it in our language. It's white. It falls from the sky like rain—and it's terribly cold. Your bones ache; all feeling goes from your hands. You can't fasten your harness and you can't feel your bowstring. Seth himself invented snow."

"Still, I would like to go," sighs Kenamun. Then he looks curiously at Senmut, who has taken a thin roll of papyrus out of his robe.

"What's that?" asks the Vizier's son.

Senmut, who still has his eyes on Nofret, who is surrounded by a group of young girls, replies, "I'll tell you later. Oh good, the dancers are coming. Is Mutardis still in the house?"

"Oh, yes," replies the young man. "My father still dotes on her. I think she's getting a bit fat."

"Shhh!" warns Senmut, as from the far end of the columned hall a group of singers and musicians enters.

"It's all right," says Kenamun. "These are only the men. *She* comes on later."

The musicians come to the center of the floor; they are all men, wearing the familiar white kilt, with ornaments on their breasts and arms. Some carry instruments— a harp, lyres, several flutes, and small square drums. The instrumentalists seat themselves on the floor. The flutes begin to wail, the harp and lyres pluck out the accompaniment, while the palms of the drummers keep up a rhythmic patter.

They sing songs in honor of the god, Amun-Re. No doubt Rekhmire, knowing that the High Priest of Amun would be present, has arranged this.

"How happy is the temple of Amun, even she that spendeth her days in festivity with the King of the Gods within her.

"She is like a woman drunken, who sitteth outside the chamber, with loosened hair. . . ."

At this point Meryet interrupts her conversation with the Mayor's wife to remark, "Look. Nozme's getting drunk again."

It is true. The plump wife of the Chief Gardener of Pharaoh has already drunk more wine than is good for her. Many of the other guests also are highly exhilarated, but

poor Nozme is nearing the point of collapse. She sways
back in her seat, laughing loudly and immoderately. Her
wig has slipped to one side and her eye paint has run. The
guests near her laugh with her, and a slave refills her cup,
which almost falls from her hand. No one, not even Meryet,
is shocked. One is expected to get drunk at parties. But
Nozme always reaches the point of intoxication quicker
than anyone else. A slave stands near her, watching her
closely, a bowl in his hand.

Now the male singers have retired and a new group of
musicians enters. This time the instrumentalists are young
girls, clad in little but fringed loincloths and a few beads.
There are two singers, a young man and a young girl. They
go through a few dancing movements, the man advancing
on the girl, kneeling with arms outstretched while she
pretends to run away. He turns his back, hides his head in
his hands, and she comes tripping back. He turns, rises, and
sings to her while the girl accompanists play a plaintive
tune on their flutes and lyres:

> "The love of the sister is upon yonder side
> A stretch of water is between us,
> And a crocodile waits on the sandbank.
> But when I go down into the water
> I tread upon the flood;
> My heart is courageous upon the waters
> And the water is like land to my feet. . . ."

A hush has fallen on the audience. They sit, with their
wine cups in their hands, looking sentimentally at the

singer. Some have their arms round their companions. In the dark corners couples are embracing.

"Her love it is that makes me strong;
    Yes, it makes water-spell for me. . . .
    I see my sister [3] coming and my heart rejoices."

Sinuhe, the young son of the Chief Secretary and Tiyi, is sitting beside his parents. He looks across the lighted hall, past the singers, to the group surrounding the Vizier. A pair of dark eyes are looking straight at him, those of Ta-kha'et. When he returns her glance, she looks away and begins to toy with the lotus flower which she holds in her slim fingers. But Sinuhe does not take his eyes away.

"I see my sister coming and my heart rejoices
    My arms are opened wide to embrace her
    And my heart rejoices upon its place. . . .
    When the mistress comes to me
    If I embrace her and her arms are opened
    It is for me as if I were one that is from Punt [4] . . ."

The male singer ends his song. There is a burst of clapping. Then the flutes and the lyres strike up again and the girl singer advances with shy, coquettish movements. She sings to the boy:

[3] In Egyptian love songs the words "sister" and "brother" simply mean "beloved" and do not necessarily denote blood relationship.
[4] The land of perfumes.

"My brother, it is pleasant to go to the pool
  In order to bathe me in thy presence,
  That I may let thee see my beauty in my tunic of finest
    royal linen
  When it is wet. . . .
  I go down with you into the water.
  And come forth again with a red fish
  Which lies beautiful on my fingers.
  Come and look at me. . . ."

But at this point there is a sudden uproar. Nozme has slipped from her chair. As her husband helps her to her feet, she has a swift attack of nausea. Some of the nearby guests laugh. A slave rushes forward with a bowl. Nozme lunges forward, misses her footing, and sprawls across the floor, knocking over the charcoal brazier which stands at the end of the room to give warmth (for the night has now grown cold). The glowing coals scatter across the floor. One of the ladies screams and draws back, upsetting her chair. The slaves rush forward, and so do some of the guests, including Sinuhe, whose parents do not notice his absence in the confusion.

But Sinuhe is not interested in putting out the fire. He reaches the pillar which screens him from the Vizier and his wife. Ta-kha'et, who has also darted out to watch the scene, is suddenly beside him. Without a word he takes her in his arms and kisses her. It is all over in a second. She struggles from his grasp and returns to her parents, while the young man goes slowly back to his chair on the other side of the hall. But it is all right. Even Tiyi has not noticed anything.

But one person has noticed—Nofret, Ta-kha'et's elder sister. She is sitting a little apart from her parents, surrounded by other young girls of good family, with whom she has spent the entire evening discussing dress, court gossip, and men. Unlike her companions, Nofret is not greatly interested in men as such; only in the offices they hold. It is not that she is mercenary; she has no need to be. She is the daughter of the Vizier and a priestess of Amun, privileged to walk before the Pharaoh himself when he enters the Temple of the King of Gods. All her life she has been surrounded by the high officers of the King, the chosen instruments of the royal power. When she marries, as, sooner or later she must, it will be some such official.[5] He will be a great man, and her children, when she has them, will be destined also for high office. That is why the action of Ta-kha'et puzzled her. Sinuhe, who was he? A handsome youth, of good family, not without talent, but of small account in the affairs of state. She could have had twenty such; men like Senmut over there, the young officer of charioteers, looking at her with his melancholy eyes. The fool! Who ever heard of a Vizier's daughter marrying a mere Army officer?

As for love, the concubines looked after that—women like Mutardis, her father's favorite. And at that moment the dancer enters, accompanied by a group of lovely young girls, naked except for brief loincloths and the beaded ornaments which adorn their breasts, arms, and ankles. Some carry tambourines, others lutes. They wear flowers in their dark hair, and their eyes are heavily painted.

The guests clap and lean forward in their chairs, as

[5] Warning to romantics. He could be her brother, or even her father.

79

Mutardis herself glides into the center of the hall. She is about thirty, and her skin is darker than that of most of her companions, for she has Nubian blood. Her black wig, falling to her shoulders, frames a masklike face of impassive beauty. Expressionless even during her most voluptuous movements, her features seem to share none of the provocation of her body. She dances with slow, serpentine movements, weaving her hips to the rhythm of the music, accenting it occasionally with a clack-clack of the castanets which she holds in her hands. She flings back her head, letting the black curls hang, then flings them forward over her eyes. Her arms outstretched, she sinks to her knees, then slowly rises again with a vibrating movement of her whole body. Meanwhile, the chorus of girls sings an ancient song:

"Sweet of love is the daughter of the King!
  Black are her tresses as the blackness of the night,
  Black as the wine-grapes are the clusters of her hair,
  The hearts of the women turn towards her with delight,
  Gazing on her beauty with which none can compare.

"Sweet of love is the daughter of the King!
  Fair are her arms in the softly swaying dance,
  Fairer by far is her bosom's rounded swell!
  The hearts of the men are as water at her glance,
  Fairer is her beauty than mortal tongue can tell. . . ."

Rekhmire watches, leaning forward in his chair, intent. Tiyi remarks to her meek husband, "One would never think she had had four children by him." Senmut, his chin resting on his cupped hands, remembers a dancer he knew in

Kadesh. Nofret looks on, detached and indifferent. This was the sort of thing men liked.

"Sweet of love is the daughter of the King!
Rose are her cheeks as the jasper's ruddy hue,
Rose as the henna which stains her slender hands!
The heart of the King is filled with love anew,
When in all her beauty before his throne she stands." [6]

The dance is over. With a final frenzy of castanets and drums, Mutardis glides backward out of the hall, her head bowed, her black curls falling over her face. The guests stamp and clap their hands. Nozme almost falls off her chair again and is saved by her husband. Meryet looks at her husband, who smiles and looks away.

And now it is near the end of the feast. Led by two young slaves, an aged harper enters the hall, bowing to right and left. He is blind, and for many years has been in Rekhmire's service. He knows the ancient songs which have been sung in Egypt for a thousand years. His father was a harper, and his father before him. He takes his seat in the place of honor beside his lord, and tunes his instrument. While this is happening, Senmut leans forward and hands to Kenamun the roll of papyrus which he has been holding all evening.

"Please give this to Nofret when I have gone," he says, not daring to look into his friend's eyes. Kenamun slips the roll into his tunic and makes no comment.

Now, at the end of the feast, comes the song which has been sung at Egyptian banquets for untold centuries,

[6] Translation by Arthur Weigall.

and which is recorded in many tombs. It expresses all too clearly the inner doubt which the Egyptians felt about the afterlife for which they so carefully prepared. The Chief Priest thinks it is a little impious, but Rekhmire likes it. After a few preliminary strokes across the strings, the harper begins:

"Bodies pass away and others remain since time of them
    that were before.
The gods that were aforetime rest in their pyramids, and
    likewise the noble and the glorified, buried in their
    pyramids.
They that build houses, their habitations are no more.
What hath been done with them?"

A silence has settled on the guests. Rekhmire's mind is far away, thinking of the deserted monuments which he passed on his way upriver; the pyramid of Cheops, of Chephren, of Djoser. . . .

"I have heard the discourses of Imhotep and Hardedef with
    whose words men speak everywhere.
What are their habitations now?
Their walls are destroyed, their habitations are no more, as
    if they had never been.

"None cometh from thence that he may tell us how they fare, that he may tell us what they need, that he may set our heart at rest, until we also go to the place whither they are gone."

Senmut, hazy with wine, his head sunk on his chest, feels the ultimate pagan pessimism, a pessimism that has nothing to do with his unavailing love for Nofret. Is this all that life has to offer? Is this the ultimate summation of the splendor of Egypt, the achievement of his ancestors, the glory of their monuments? A round of sensuality ending in final extinction? The harper sings on, but his words bring no comfort to Senmut.

"Be glad, that thou mayest cause thine year to forget that men will one day beautify thee.
Follow thy desire, so long as thou livest.
Put myrrh on thy head, clothe thee in fine linen, and annoint thee with the genuine marvels of the things of the God.
Increase yet more the delights that thou hast, and let not thy heart grow faint.
Follow thy desire, and do good to thyself.
Do what thou requirest upon earth and vex not thine heart—until that day of lamentation comes to thee.
Yet He with the Quiet Heart [7] hears not their lamentation, and cries deliver no man from the Underworld."

The song ends; the guests rise to go. They say good-bye to their host and hostess and, preceded by slaves with torches, make their way unsteadily along the passage which leads to the porter's lodge. There the chariots are waiting, the drivers at their posts, the runners standing ready. The moon rides high over the palm trees, and the torches which

[7] Osiris.

accompany the first guests to depart are already a faint glimmer in the distance.

In the almost empty hall, Nofret is reading the papyrus roll which her brother has given her from Senmut. It is an old poem, beautifully set out in hieratic by one of the best scribes in Thebes:

Seven days from yesterday I have not seen my beloved,
And sickness has crept over me,
And I am become heavy in my limbs
And am unmindful of mine own body.
If the master-physicians come to me,
My heart has no comfort of their remedies,
And the magicians, no resource is in them,
My malady is not diagnosed.

Better for me is my beloved than any remedies,
More important is she for me than the entire compendium
    of medicine.

    My salutation is when she enters from without.
    When I see her, then am I well;
    Opens she her eye, my limbs are young again;
    Speaks she, and I am strong;
    And when I embrace her, she banishes evil,
    And it passes from me for seven days.

Nofret, the open scroll in her hand, walks slowly over to the brazier and drops it on the glowing coals. She watches it as it flares up, curls, and sinks in ashes. Then, accompanied by her slaves, she walks to the women's quarters.

# CHAPTER 5

# THE EGYPTIAN WOMAN

W ITH the exception of Rekhmire and his family (whose names are known from his tomb), and Amenemhab, all the characters in the foregoing chapters were invented, but their prototypes can be recognized in Ancient Egyptian literature and tomb inscriptions. All I have done is put them together in a common setting, let them react upon one another, and develop a life of their own. At the same time I can assure anyone reading this book for factual information that he is not being led astray by a flight of undisciplined imagination. Every incident I have described could have happened, and several did happen. The prototype of Rekhmire's house can be seen in Theban tomb paintings, represented to the last detail: the porter's lodge, the garden, the three passages, the hall of columns, the harem, and the servants' quarters with the rooms peopled by the men and women who occupied them in life. You can see such a picture in the tomb of Ay, at Tell-el-Amarna, and there are other examples. Pictures of feasts occur frequently in Egyptian tombs, and most of the details of Rekhmire's feast have been taken from scenes in his own tomb. There you may still see the musicians, the dancing girls, and the guests holding lotus flowers, watching the entertainment while slaves hand them food and drink.

That children sometimes attended such feasts is proved

by the fact that one of the tomb frescoes at Tell-el-Amarna shows the small daughters of Akhnaten and Nefretiti sitting beside their parents' chairs. And even Nebet's toy horse has its prototype, found in a tomb. In another Theban tomb you can see Nozme getting drunk and vomiting into a bowl held by a slave. In another a blind harper is shown, and above his figure is the very song which I have put into the mouth of Rekhmire's singer. All the songs are authentic: the love songs, the hymns to Amun-Re, and the song to which Mutardis danced. Some of these were found on papyri of an earlier or later date than the period we are describing, but there is no reason to suppose that these songs, or others like them, were not sung in the time of Rekhmire. As for the Vizier himself and his beautiful wife, their portraits can be seen to this day in a Theban tomb which is one of the most interesting in the Necropolis. In one of these scenes he is shown disembarking from a boat after a voyage to Middle Egypt. Many other scenes from his life are depicted on the walls of his tomb, and some of these will be described in later chapters. We shall also meet again Nofret, Sinuhe and Ta-kha'et, Kenamun and Senmut, in different settings.

It may be objected, by readers who come fresh to the study of Ancient Egypt, that the women in Rekhmire's house seem to enjoy a status higher than might be expected in an Oriental country. In this, however, they would be wrong. One of the most attractive and human aspects of Ancient Egyptian life, and one which brings them very close to us, was their affectionate family life. Among the educated classes women seem to have been honored and respected. Many tomb inscriptions and many letters which have come down to us bear witness to the love and respect which the Egyptian bore towards his womenfolk. One of the precepts of the great sage 'Eney was:

> Thou shalt never forget what thy mother has done for thee. . . . She bare thee and nourished thee in all manner of ways. If thou forgettest her, she might blame thee, she might "lift up her arms to God, and He would hear her complaint." After the appointed months she bare thee, she nursed thee for three years. She brought thee up, and when thou didst enter the school, and was instructed in the writings, she came daily to thy master with bread and beer from her house.

Another wise man, Ptah-hotetp, gives the following advice:

> If thou art a man of note, found for thyself an household, and love thy wife at home, as it beseemeth. Fill her belly, clothe her back; unguent is the remedy for her limbs. Gladden her heart, as long as she lives; she is a goodly field for her lord.

However, a man could take more than one legitimate wife, and if he was rich he could keep numerous concubines as well. There are references in some inscriptions to "beautiful singers" and other attendants in "the house of the women." But the chief wife always held precedence; she is shown in the tomb paintings in company with her husband, feasting or hunting, helping to supervise his estate, or receiving tribute. She is referred to as "his beloved wife" or "his darling," and many of the personal names of women speak eloquently of their husbands' affection—such names as "First Favorite," "Loving One," "My Mistress Is as Gold," and "This Is My Queen." [1]

Another significant fact is that, whereas in some Oriental lands the male children were more important than the female (as among the Arabs today), in Ancient Egypt the names given to the daughters show that they were held in equal honor. Some of these names are touching; there is "Beauty Comes," "Ruler of Her Father," and—rather oddly—"Beautiful as Her Father." To me the most moving of all is the name evidently given by a father to his daughter after his wife had died—perhaps in childbirth. It is "Replace Her."

Sons also were given similarly affectionate names: "Riches Come," "His Father Lives," and—clearly a soldier's infant son—"Chief of the Mercenaries." Other names which could apply equally to boys or girls are "My Own," "I Have Wished It," "Acceptable," and "Welcome." [2]

There is a papyrus at Leyden in Holland which contains a letter written by a widower to his dead wife, breathing an affection and tenderness which touches our hearts, even over a distance of three thousand years. After his wife's death the bereaved husband was struck down with illness. Some priest or magician seems to have told him that his misfortune was due to neglect of his wife during life.

---

[1] A particular favorite of mine is "She is Healthy."

[2] However, other names suggest considerably less joy at the arrival of the offspring: *e.g.*, Kison ("Another Brother!"); Nenneka ("No Use"); Nendisy ("I Won't Give Her!"); Entensu ("He's Yours!"); and Nehehendisn ("Eternity for Him Who Gave Him!").

" 'Anch'ere, the dead wife," said the magician, "was angry with her husband, and he must write her a letter to propitiate her grieved spirit." The widower, who was probably a good husband, responded to this cruel advice by writing a letter full of bewilderment, pain, and love:

> What evil have I done to you, that I should find myself in this wretched state? What then have I done to you, that you should lay your hand upon me, when no evil was done to you? You became my wife when I was young, and I was with you. I was appointed to all manner of offices, and I was with you. I did not forsake you or cause your heart any sorrow. . . . Behold, when I commanded the foot-soldiers of Pharaoh, together with his chariot force, I did cause you to come that they might fall down before you, and they brought all manner of good things to present to you. . . . When you were ill with the sickness which afflicted you, I went to the Chief Physician and he made you your medicine, he did everything that you said he should do. When I had to accompany Pharaoh on his journey to the south, my thoughts were with you, and I spent those eight months without caring to eat or drink. When I returned to Memphis, I besought Pharaoh and betook myself to you, and I greatly mourned for you with the people of my house.

Evidently 'Anch'ere died while her husband was on foreign service.

On the other hand, one must avoid oversentimentaliz-

ing the Egyptian's marital relations. He may have been a
kind and devoted husband, but he was rarely monogamous
if he could afford to be otherwise. Kings and nobles kept
large harems, as do some Oriental princes today. In the
tomb of Ay, already mentioned, can be seen a detailed representation of the owner's harem, with the bored eunuchs
lounging at the doors of the women's chambers, the occupants of which are making up their faces, dressing each
other's hair and practicing dances and songs for the entertainment of their master. Most of these women were probably slaves and did not find any degradation in their position; in fact, it was an honor for a woman to "find favor
in the eyes of her lord." The children of such women were
brought up in the harem, but the children of the chief wife
probably had precedence. Also, the slaves and concubines
had no legal status and could be dismissed at will.

Woman in all her aspects can be recognized in the
pages of Egyptian literature: the devoted wife, the good
mother, the passionate young girl, the prostitute, the
"floozy," and the seductress. The last-named type occurs
frequently, and warnings against her wiles are given in the
Wisdom Books, the reputed sayings of such wise men as
Imhotep, 'Eney, and Ptah-hotetp:

> Beware of a woman from strange parts, whose
> city is not known. When she comes do not look at her
> or know her. She is as the eddy in deep water, the
> depth of which is unknown. The woman whose hus-
> band is far off writes to thee every day. If no witness
> is near her she stands up and spreads out her net. O
> fearful crime to listen to her!

To avoid falling into such snares young men were advised to marry early and beget children, the possession of which was considered the greatest happiness. "Thy wife will present thee with a son like unto thyself."

The high status which "respectable" women enjoyed in Ancient Egypt arose in part from the matriarchal system, on which the family was based. All landed property descended in the female line from mother to daughter. When a man married an heiress, he enjoyed her property only as long as his wife lived. On her death it passed to her daughter and her daughter's husband. This practice was never more strictly observed than in the Royal Family, which explains why so many of the Pharaohs married their sisters, or even their infant daughters. Often these marriages were purely formal affairs. Margaret Murray in *The Splendour That Was Egypt* says:

> The marriage laws of Ancient Egypt were never formulated, and knowledge of them can be obtained only by working out the marriages and genealogies. It then becomes evident that a Pharaoh safeguarded himself from abdication by marrying every heiress without any regard to consanguinity, so that if the chief heiress died, he was already married to the next in succession and thus retained the sovereignty . . . the throne went strictly in the female line. The great wife of the king was the heiress; by right of marriage with her, the king came to the throne. The king's birth was not important. He might be of any rank, but if he married the queen he at once became king; the queen was queen by right of birth, the king by right of marriage.

This custom of matrilineal descent explains the marriages of Cleopatra. She first married her eldest brother, whose right to the throne was thus established. When he died, Cleopatra married her younger brother, who ruled by right of this marriage. There were no children by either of these unions. When Caesar conquered Egypt, he in turn had to marry Cleopatra to make his accession legal in the eyes of the Egyptian people. Next came Marc Antony, who by marrying Cleopatra secured the throne. She had a son by Caesar, a son and daughter by Antony. When Antony fell and Octavius arrived, he too was ready to espouse the much-married Queen, but, as Margaret Murray says, "she wisely preferred death."

Affinity was obviously no bar to marriage in Ancient Egypt. Queens often married their brothers, and sometimes kings their daughters, *e.g.,* Snofru, Rameses II, and Amenophis IV (Akhnaten). This was done to maintain the purity of the royal blood and keep the inheritance within the ruling family, but the practice was probably less common among the Pharaoh's subjects. However, even as late as Roman times Diodorus could write, "It was a law in Egypt, against the custom of all other nations, that brothers and sisters might marry one with another." The Romans used to say, "You may go halfway to Athens [the Greeks permitted marriage with a half sister], the whole way to Alexandria."

It is sometimes thought that consanguineous marriages produce mental or physical defects in the children. This does not necessarily happen—in fact, the practice can improve the stock. The trouble occurs when, after generations of inbreeding, a defect in either parent may result in a deformed or imbecile offspring. This is probably what happened at the end of the Eighteenth Dynasty. The "heretic Pharaoh," Akhnaten, though intellectually brilliant, was physically malformed, and his successor, Tutankhamun, died while still a youth.

The custom of female inheritance gave the women of Egypt considerable power. Petrie writes:

> The ancestors are always traced farther back in the female than the male line. The father was only the holder of office, the mother was the family link. . . . The same in respect of property; that goes through the *nebt per,* the mistress of the house; we never find a *neb per* or master of the house.

Marriage contracts which have survived show that the woman's rights were well respected. In a contract dating from 580 B.C., but probably based on earlier contracts, the prospective husband takes oath that if he leaves his wife "either from dislike, or preferring another (apart from the great crime which is found in women)," he will return the dowry and a share of all paternal and maternal property for the children which she may bear.

Another marriage contract, somewhat later in date, contains the lines: "I establish thee as wife. If I neglect thee, or take any other wife than thee, I shall give thee . . . [here follows a sum of money]." The same contractor agrees that half his father's property, which his mother gave him "and the rest of the contracts coming from her . . . shall belong to thee, as well as the ensuing rights." [3]

[3] Petrie, *Social Life in Ancient Egypt.*

If the marriage failed, divorce was easy. The formula for the man was to say before duly accredited witnesses, "I have abandoned thee as wife. I am removed from thee. I have no claim on earth upon thee. I have said unto thee, 'Make for thyself a husband in any place to which thou shalt go.' " At the same time, financial provision had to be made for the divorced wife. Similarly, a wife wishing to divorce her husband also had to pay compensation:

> If she shall stand up in the congregation and shall say, "I divorce my husband," the price of divorce shall be on her head; she shall return to the scales and weigh for Ashor [the husband] five shekels, and all which I have delivered into her hand she shall give back, and she shall go away whithersoever she will.[4]

There is no evidence that marriage was ever regarded as indissoluble, or that any religious ceremony was connected with it. It was purely a civil contract, with a heavy fine imposed on the person breaking it.

As in most countries at most times, marriage, childbearing, and homemaking were the principal occupations of Egyptian women. The few professions open to them were the priesthood, midwifery, dancing, and mourning. Young women entering the priesthood had to learn the sacred songs and dances, but this was not a religious vocation as we understand the term, and they were under no vows of celibacy. Secular dancers belonged to a highly skilled professional class, probably drawn from a lower

---

[4] Marriage contract between Jews living at Elephantine, in Upper Egypt, in 442 B.C. (Petrie's translation).

level of society than that of the temple dancers. Mourning is still a recognized profession in Egypt. In the country, during a funeral, professional mourners with disheveled hair run weeping beside the coffin as it is carried to the grave, sending up the old, wailing cry for the dead which may have descended from the time of the Pharaohs. These women too would be of the lower class.

Inevitably, when we try to present a picture of Egyptian womanhood, our view will be incomplete, since only the wives and daughters of the well to do have left us their portraits. The masses must forever remain anonymous. We see them occasionally as tiny figures in the tomb painting of some great noble, working in the fields, gleaning corn (and quarreling over the gleanings: in one picture two girls are shown pulling each other's hair), dancing for their lord, or mourning his death. Occasionally we find statuettes of women grinding corn between stone querns, just as their descendants do today. The life of the Egyptian peasant woman was a hard round of menial toil, regularly but briefly interrupted by childbirth, as in the East today. Unlike her richer sisters, she probably aged very quickly and died at a comparatively early age. Occasionally such a woman might see her son rise to high office (for this was possible in Egypt), and then she and her husband might enjoy some comfort and security in their old age—might even be given a tomb instead of a nameless grave. But for the great majority "it is as if they had never been."

The Ancient Egyptians have left no novels, and their histories are mainly dull chronicles of wars and conquests. We shall look in vain for the character sketches of Egyptian women such as enable us to picture a Zenobia, an Aspasia, or a Poppaea. Cleopatra lives in the pages of Plutarch, but she was a Ptolemy, and her blood owed as much to the chieftains of Macedonia as to the daughters of the Nile. The women of Ancient Egypt are even more baffling than the rest of their sex, since so little is known about them. And yet so long as the lovely portrait head of Nefretiti exists, men will never cease to wonder and speculate. How gratified these ladies would be if they knew that after three thousand, four thousand, five thousand years they could still arouse admiration!

Perhaps part of the secret of their charm is the fact that, after many revolutions in the male conception of female beauty, the Ancient Egyptian woman approximates more closely the current feminine ideal than the beauties of classical, medieval, and Renaissance times. The slim fifteenth-century ladies with their tiny waists and narrow, flowing skirts conform to modern fashion, but their faces are cold and remote; they clasp missals in their slim hands and their thoughts seem to be set above earthly things. The Rubensesque women of the seventeenth century, exposing masses of generous flesh, are perhaps a little too lusty and earthy for our jaded palates. The beauties of Greece and Rome arouse our admiration, but do not excite us. They seem as cold as the marble from which they are hewn. But put Nefretiti in a Dior gown and she could enter a fashionable restaurant and be instantly accepted. Even her make-up would not arouse comment.

But much as I admire Nefretiti, my own personal favorites are represented in two pictures which hang in the room in which I write and are reproduced in this book.

The first is the lovely frieze of young girls going in procession before Pharaoh, found by Zakaria Goneim in the tomb of Kheruef, a noble of the Eighteenth Dynasty. One of these girls could have been Nofret. The picture is reproduced on Plate 18. The other, shown on Plate 20 represents a goddess and stands in the Egyptian Museum in Cairo. Every time I visit this museum I always make a point of studying this lovely piece of sculpture. I do not know who she is: I have never bothered to find out. But to me, who am only one among her many admirers, she represents the type of Egyptian woman of whom some long-dead admirer wrote:

She is profitable of speech, agreeable in her conversation, of good counsel in her writings; all that passes her lips is like the work of the Goddess of Truth, a perfect woman, greatly praised in her city, giving the hand to all, saying that which is good, repeating what one loves, giving pleasure to all, nothing evil has ever passed her lips, most beloved by all. . . .

# CHAPTER 6

# LOVERS AND FRIENDS

I T is not difficult to draw appropriate parallels between life in Ancient Egypt and life in the present day. Nonetheless, we must admit, if we are honest, that the career of an Egyptian lawyer or administrator was not exactly like that of his modern counterpart; nor was the life of an Egyptian soldier campaigning in Syria precisely like that of a G.I. in Korea or a British infantryman in Malaya. But there is one important human activity we share with the Ancient Egyptians which draws us so close to them that the centuries melt away, and that is love. The passion and tenderness of Egyptian love poems can still move sympathetic hearts, though the warm limbs which inspired them have long since crumbled to dust, and scholars now ponder over lines which were written only for the eyes of lovers.

Ta-kha'et and Sinuhe could meet only rarely, and then usually under parental supervision. But young people can always find ways of meeting, and the love poems which have come down to us betray a knowledge of human passion which is recognizable immediately by anyone who has been in love. However, for the moment we will assume that they are separated.

The young girl, Ta-kha'et, is entertaining some of her friends in the garden of her parents' house. They lie under the sycamore trees beside a shady pool while slaves serve them with food and drink and others sing and dance for their entertainment. Ta-kha'et, in a fine linen gown, a garland of flowers around her shoulders, reclines lazily on one elbow listening to the song, which is called "The Flowers in the Garden":

"*Mekmekh*-flowers! Thou makest the heart equable. I do unto thee that which thou desireth, when I am in thine arms.

"My chief request is paint for mine eye, and my seeing thee is light for mine eyes. I nestle close to thee, because I see thy love, thou man, for whom most I crave.

"How pleasant is mine hour! Might an hour only become for me eternity, when I sleep with thee. Thou didst lift up mine heart . . . when it was night.

"*Seamu*-flowers are in it! One is made great in their presence. I am thy first sister.

"I am unto thee like a garden, which I have planted with flowers and all manner of sweet-smelling herbs.

"Pleasant is the channel in it, which thine hand hath digged, at the cooling of the north wind. The beautiful place where I walk about, when thine hand resteth in mine, and mine heart is satisfied with joy, because we walk together.

"*Shedeh* is it, my hearing of thy voice, and I live because I hear it. Whenever I see thee, it is better for me than food and drink.

"*Zait*-flowers are in it! I take thy chaplets, when

thou comest drunken and thou liest on thy bed. I will stroke thy feet. . . ."

The guests show their appreciation as the song ends. Slaves refill the wine cups, and another singer begins her song. She takes the part of a sycamore tree, talking to the maiden who lies beneath its shade:

"The little sycamore, which she hath planted with her hand, it moveth its mouth to speak. The whispering of its leaves is as sweet as refined honey. How charming are its pretty branches, verdant as. . . . It is laden with *neku*-fruits, that are redder than jasper. Its leaves are like unto malachite, and are . . . as glass. . . .

"It slippeth a letter into the hand of a little maid, the daughter of its chief gardener, and maketh her run to the beloved: 'Come, and pass the time in the midst of thy maiden! The garden is in its day. There are bowers and shelters there for thee. My gardeners are glad and rejoice when they see thee. Send thy slaves ahead of thee, supplied with utensils. Of a truth one is already drunken when one hasteneth to thee, ere one hath yet drunken! But the servants come from thee with their vessels, and bring beer of every sort and all manner of mixed loaves, and many flowers of yesterday and to-day, and all manner of refreshing fruit.

" 'Come, and spend the day in merriment, and tomorrow, and the day after, three whole days, and sit in my shadow.'

"Her lover sitteth on her right hand. She maketh

him drunken, and heedeth all he said. The feast is dis-
ordered with drunkenness, and she stayeth on with
her brother.

"But I am discreet, and speak not of what I see. I
will say no word. . . ."

Meanwhile, in his father's house, Sinuhe, who, like all
educated Egyptian men, has learned to read, is engrossed
in a roll of papyrus. He is studying for the priesthood, and
his sharp-eyed father, who is at the moment resting on his
bed under the colonnade, thinks that his son is studying the
sacred writings. He would probably be outraged if he could
see what Sinuhe is actually reading:

"If I kiss her and her lips are open, I am happy
even without beer. . . . I say to you (a handmaiden),
'Put the finest linen between her limbs, make not her
bed with royal linen, and beware of white linen. Adorn
her couch with . . . and sprinkle it with *tishepes* oil.'

"Ah, would I were her Negress that is her hand-
maid, then would I behold the colour of her limbs.

"Ah, would I were the washerman. . . . In a
single month I would wash out the unguents which
are in her clothing.

"Ah, would I were her signet ring which is on
her finger. . . ."

The sun is sinking; the shadows of the trees in
Ta-kha'et's garden grow longer; and a breeze has sprung up,
faintly rippling the surface of the ornamental pool. The
sound of lutes and harps comes faintly across the water,

mingled with the chatter and laughter of the young girls. Now a girl is singing a duet with a male singer. First, the girl sings:

"If thou desireth to caress my thigh, my breast will comfort thee.

"Wilt thou go away because thou hast besought thee of eating? Art thou a glutton?

"Wilt thou go away and clothe thyself? But I have a sheet.

"Wilt thou go away because thou art thirsty? Take to thee my breast; what it hath overfloweth for thee.

"The love of thee penetrateth my body . . . like the love-apple. . . ."

The young man replies:

"Her breast is one with love-apples. Her brow is the bird-trap of Meru-wood, and I am the goose which is snared by the worm."

And his partner again takes up the song:

"Hath not mine heart compassion on thy love for me? I will not let go of thy love, even if I am beaten . . . as far as the land of Palestine with shebet and clubs, and unto the land of Ethiopia with palm-ribs, as far as the hill with sticks, and unto the field with cudgels. I will not heed their designs, so as to forsake love. . . ."

However, not all the youth of Thebes are spending their time reading or listening to love poems in the secluded gardens of the great. For example, Kenamun, the son of Rekhmire, has obtained his father's permission to go on a hunting party with his friend Senmut and a number of other young noblemen. The party set out several days ago for the hunting grounds in the high desert behind the Theban hills. For the past two nights they have pitched their tents in the desert and marched during the day, and now they are arrived at the place where they hope to find sport. Lions and leopards are known to inhabit the district, but Senmut is doubtful if they will be found. "If we find a few gazelle or an ibex," he says, "we shall be lucky."

Kenamun, the younger man, is more optimistic, but in any case he is less interested in a successful day's hunting than in being able to talk to Senmut, the young officer of chariotry, whom he hero-worships. In the early morning as the rising sun reddens the desert sand, they wait near a low ridge, while the beaters erect a light network of fences into which they will drive the game. The two young men sit opposite each other on the ground, Kenamun admiringly fingering the great bow which Senmut has carried on his campaigns in Syria. Their servants stand ready with quivers full of arrows.

"My father says," says Kenamun, "that One [1] will be returning to the land of the Mountain-dwellers, perhaps in the spring."

"I have heard talk of it."

"May Amun give strength to his arm."

Senmut nods, smiles, but says nothing.

[1] Pharaoh.

"Why do you smile?" asks Kenamun.

"Because the Mountain-dwellers too have powerful gods."

"But Amun was triumphant!"

"Menkheperre [2] was triumphant. If he had not been the great soldier he is, Amun couldn't have helped us."

Kenamun laughs. "You'd better not let my father hear you say that," he says.

"Or Nofret?"

"Nofret wouldn't even understand you."

"But she's a priestess."

"Yes; but only because my father has made her become one. She's not interested in anything or anyone but herself."

"You're hard on your sister, Kenamun."

"I tell you, you're wasting your time," replies the younger man. "I didn't mean to tell you this, but you may as well know. She burned your precious poem."

Senmut stands up, takes the bow from Kenamun's hands and slings a quiver over his shoulder. "They're coming," he says, and runs up the sandy ridge, followed by Kenamun.

From the desert comes the distant baying of hounds and the loud cries of the beaters. The two huntsmen, with their companions, wait on the ridge, shielding their eyes from the glare of the sun. Beside each sportsman stand their attendants, waiting to hand a fresh quiver of arrows to their masters as the first is exhausted.

Suddenly two gazelles appear out of the haze, racing across the desert towards the enclosure which, unknown to

[2] One of the names of the Pharaoh Tuthmosis III.

them, had been prepared for their destruction. Senmut grasps his bow, sinks onto one knee, and pulls the arrow back to the head. Before he can release it, the excited Kenamun has let fly his shaft, which goes wide; the Vizier's son lets out an oath which would have earned a sharp reproof from his father. As he reaches for another arrow, there is a loud twang from Senmut's bow and in a second the first gazelle falls in its tracks, sending up a flurry of sand.

"Try for the second one!" shouts Senmut. But again Kenamun's arrow fails to reach its mark.

"You'll have to shoot better than that in Syria!" laughs his friend.

Together they hurry down the slope with the other sportsmen, as, from the north, a cloud of sand races towards them, a cloud which gradually splits into thirty or forty scurrying shapes: a group of terrified animals—ibexes, gazelles, hares—which are fleeing before the approaching hounds.

The bowstrings hum; the long arrows soar through the air. There is a babel of excited voices, of huntsmen, beaters, and servants encouraging their masters, all mixed with the loud baying of the hounds.

Seven more gazelles lie lifeless on the sand. A wounded ibex stumbles towards the ridge, an arrow in its flank, but is dispatched by another shaft from Kenamun—the first time he has hit anything.

Suddenly Senmut hands his bow to his servant with a look of disgust.

"I'm sick of this," he says to Kenamun. "We'll go back to the camp."

Without a word, but looking curiously at his friend, Kenamun mounts his chariot and follows Senmut.

Gradually the sound of the huntsmen and hounds fades into silence, and there is nothing but the padding of hoofs on the sand, and the hard breathing of the horses. They reach the group of tents in a *wadi,* and dismount. Then Senmut speaks. "It's true—that rumor you heard. Menk-heperre *is* returning to Syria."

"When?"

"In about two months, perhaps less."

"Are you going?"

"Yes. And so are you."

Before Kenamun can express his delight, Senmut hurries on, "Your father knows about it; he'll tell you in due course. The General has won him over; you're to be transferred to my regiment. But don't think it is going to be another hunting party. You'll have to learn to march for days with little food and water; you must learn how to handle a chariot on mountain tracks. You'll have to fight an enemy whom you rarely see; an enemy who lurks behind rocks, who suddenly swoops down on you from the mountains when you're in column of route, kills a few score of your men, and then disappears before you can fit an arrow into your bow."

"But you've fought the Bedouin many times," objects Kenamun, "and you're still alive."

"Perhaps I've been lucky. And I'd rather be killed by them than captured. I've seen what they do to their prisoners. . . ."

"Then why do you want to go back to Syria? And you *do* want to go back. I know that."

Senmut thinks for a while, frowning.

"I don't think it's only the fighting," he says. "Yes, I enjoy that, too—the adventure of it, the danger. But it's more than that. I love the mountains, the strange people, the strange trees, the strange gods. And some of their women are very beautiful."

He reflects again and goes on, "No, it's not even that. You'll only understand what I mean when you leave Egypt. Once you've been out of your own land, things are never the same again. Egyptians who have always stayed at home have no curiosity about life. They think that Egypt is the world. It's not the world. The world is a much stranger place than they can ever know. Wait till you see Kadesh and Tubikhi. Wait till you see the road to Meger." [3]

"Where is that?"

"In the mountains. There the sky is dark even by day. There are oaks and cypresses and cedars which blot out the sky. There are lions and panthers and hyenas to hunt—not harmless gazelles. There's the Pass of Megiddo, a ravine two thousand cubits deep, filled with boulders and shingle, with a Bedouin behind every bush."

"Well, I shall be seeing it soon, I hope," says Kenamun.

There is a distant baying of dogs and the sound of voices. The hunting party is returning to the camp. Senmut gets up, adjusts his sword belt, then slaps his friend on the shoulder as he remarks, "If you want to live to tell your father about it, you'll have to shoot better than you did today."

[3] Probably in the Lebanon.

# CHAPTER 7

# THE PHARAOH'S ARMY

I DO not intend immediately to follow Senmut and Kenamun into Syria, because it happens that Ancient Egyptian records have survived which give a more vivid and authentic picture of warfare in Asia than anything I could invent. I shall quote these records in a later part of this chapter, but first it will be useful to consider the organization of the Pharaonic armies, not only in the time of Tuthmosis III, but in earlier and later periods. For this information I am indebted mainly to Mr. R. O. Faulkner, and readers who wish for further details should refer to his interesting article, "Egyptian Military Organisation" in Volume 39 of the *Journal of Egyptian Archaeology*.

During the Old Kingdom, when war impended, "local officials were called upon to embody and command a quota of troops from those under their authority. . . . The fully mobilised army therefore included a great many local corps of the nature of a militia, the members of which will presumably have done military service or have had a certain amount of military training." In other words, the system of recruitment was rather like the feudal system used in Europe during the Middle Ages. The only army unit mentioned in Old Kingdom texts is the "battalion." The size of this is unknown, but if, as the text states, the armies consisted of "many tens of thousands," the unit may well have been the size of one of our divisions.

The disadvantage of this system, as in medieval times, was that it put too much power into the hands of the local magnates. And when, for instance, in the Intermediate Period following the decline of the Old Kingdom there was a lack of power at the center, the provincial nobles made war upon each other and anarchy prevailed. However, there was probably a small standing army as well, under the direct command of the king. Otherwise, as Faulkner points out, it would have been difficult for the Pharaoh to cope with a sudden emergency, such as an invasion or rebellion. Therefore the king probably maintained this small force of trained troops, which were always at hand when immediate action was needed.

In Old Kingdom tombs at Sakkara and Deshabshah there are battle scenes which give the impression of well-trained and competent Egyptian troops; probably disciplined regular soldiers led the field, backed up by conscripts. Most of what we know of military organization under the Old Kingdom is derived from the chronicles of a certain Weni, who describes a force levied for campaigns in Asia. Weni does not mention a regular force but this

. . . does not imply that there was no such force. He is simply concerned to point out that all available sources of men throughout Egypt were called upon for service, and he may well have taken the small permanent nucleus of troops for granted as having to serve in any case.[1]

[1] Faulkner.

It must also be remembered that in peacetime it was usual to levy troops, not only for military duties, but to carry out public works, such as quarrying. The title "general" is applied sometimes to officials who were carrying out duties not strictly of a military nature. For example, of the generals known from the First to the Seventh Dynasties

. . . three commanded expeditions to Sinai, three led quarrying expeditions to the Wadi Hammamat, and one . . . was in charge at Turah. Of the others, Prince Kamtjenent, son of King Izezi, may perhaps have seen service abroad, one named Kherdni had authority over a whole body of new recruits, while yet another was probably stationed at Elephantine and was in command of Nubian auxiliaries.

The only regular officer whose rank is given in Old Kingdom inscriptions is "general" or "army commander," but obviously subordinate officers must have existed and indeed can be identified in the battle scenes at Sakkara and Deshabshah. They carried a staff of office to distinguish them from the rank and file.

On the Sinai tablet of King Djoser [2800 B.C.] the general carries a staff and an axe; in the battle-scene at Deshabshah the officer watching the sappers at work leans on a staff and has a dagger stuck in his belt. . . .

Conscription, which in Europe is barely a couple of centuries old, was an accepted institution during the earliest period of Egyptian history. Five thousand years ago young Egyptians of military age were called to the colors, did their specified period of military service under a local commander, and then returned to their normal occupations, though remaining liable for call-up in an emergency. During their period of service the State fed and clothed them. It is not known if they received any pay. We hear of a "General of recruits" (*i.e.*, conscripts), "controllers of recruits," and the "overseer of Palace Youths and Recruits"—presumably the household troops corresponding to our Brigade of Guards.

An important function of troops in the Old Kingdom and later periods was the garrisoning of the fortresses and blockhouses which guarded the frontiers of Egypt and the roads leading into Asia and Nubia. Their functions were rather like those of the Foreign Legion in North Africa, and the enemy they faced—the Bedouin—was the same.

During the Middle Kingdom, after the period of anarchy which followed the collapse of the Old Kingdom, the provincial governors, or *nomarchs,* wielded considerable power, and were allowed to retain their own armies. However, as in medieval times, these probably had to furnish a certain number of troops for the royal service. There was also, says Faulkner, a royal standing army, recruited by conscription; and he draws attention to a *stela* (memorial stone) which states that, in the twenty-fifth year of Ammenemes III, an Army scribe "came southward to choose recruits of the Abydos-nome of the Southern Province." On another *stela* there is a reference to Nakhtsebkre . . . "who gave one man in a hundred males to his lord, the Lord of the Falchion, when he was sent to raise a regiment of soldiers." However, 1 per cent of the male population can hardly have been a burden on the population.

From inscriptions of the Middle Kingdom we can learn a little more about Egyptian military organization. For instance, beside the title of "general" we find "commander of shock-troops" and "instructor of retainers." These "shock-troops" were probably picked men used as assault troops. The "retainers," originally nonmilitary attendants on the king, became in time his personal bodyguard charged with the protection of the king's person when he went to war. They were like the gentlemen-at-arms of medieval times, and they also seem to have officered the troops of the royal household. There is an interesting autobiographical record by one Sebekkhu, a soldier who lived in the time of Sesostris III, which shows how a young cadet could rise in rank as he gained experience.

When Sesostris III came to the throne, Sebekkhu was appointed "warrior of the bodyguard," with a little squad of seven men; later he became "retainer of *the* Ruler" (*i.e.*, the King), commanding sixty men. He took part in the Pharaoh's Nubian campaigns with six other royal retainers, and on his return home was promoted to be "instructor of retainers," with a command of one hundred men. Since only seven of these "retainers" accompanied the King on this expedition, they were probably young officers of high birth.

The administrative side of the Army was looked after by the "Army scribes"; there were many of these military clerks, and one comes across them constantly in records of campaigns. They too had various grades of rank, from the junior who looked after the affairs of a small detachment to the senior who had charge of the administration of a whole corps; their modern equivalents would be found in the Royal Army pay corps and the quartermaster's stores. But in Ancient Egypt they were also responsible for the conscription of young men liable for service.

However, it is not until we study the records of the New Empire, the period in which most of the action of this book is set, that we can find really detailed accounts of army organization and administration and, more important, personal records of campaigns, which give us a vivid picture of what it was like to fight in the Pharaoh's wars.

Under the Eighteenth Dynasty the Egyptians became for the first and only time a truly military people. In a way this situation can be compared with the triumphs of the French Army following on the French Revolution and the subsequent rise of Napoleon. After the collapse of the Middle Kingdom, Egypt was invaded by Asiatic barbarians, the Hyksos, or "Shepherd-Kings." They were finally driven out by warrior-princes from Thebes, whose successors founded the Eighteenth Dynasty. And with the Eighteenth Dynasty the military glory of Egypt begins. Determined to make their country safe from any future invasion from Asia, these Eighteenth Dynasty kings, Ahmosis, Amenophis I, Amenophis II, and the various Tuthmoses, penetrated into Palestine and Syria, subduing the country and establishing strong garrisons there. The greatest of these kings, the "Napoleon of Ancient Egypt," was Tuthmosis III, who extended the dominion of Egypt as far as the Euphrates. Looking at the shriveled face of this great King in the Cairo Museum (see illustration on Plate 43), it is difficult to recognize that this was the one military genius whom Ancient Egypt produced.

The Pharaoh was head of the Army, and usually took command in the field. The Vizier corresponded to a modern Minister of War, assisted by an Army Council, to whom he gave his orders. But in the field the King consulted his principal officers immediately before an engagement. At this time too the King maintained a large standing army which was organized on a national basis and officered by professional soldiers. Faulkner writes:

> The actual field army was organised in divisions, each of which was a complete army corps consisting of both chariotry and infantry and numbering about 5,000 men; at Kadesh [a famous battlefield of Rameses II] the divisional commanders were apparently royal princes, though one division was led by the Pharaoh in person. These divisions were named after the principal gods of the realm.

The two principal arms of the service were infantry and chariotry. An interesting fact is that there was as yet no cavalry, probably because the breed of horses developed at that time was too weak in the back to stand up to hard military riding. The chariot itself was a relatively new arm, introduced by the invading Hyksos, and was used much as tanks and armored vehicles are used in modern warfare— as a screen behind which the infantry could advance. As Faulkner says:

> In a field action it was the chariotry which took the first shock of battle, the infantry advancing behind them to exploit a tactical success or to stem the

enemy's advance if matters went awry. . . . The chariotry also charged the enemy at the moment of victory, so as to turn a defeat into rout, and it is doubtless this phase that we see in those familiar pictures where Pharaoh charges in his chariot over a carpet of dead and dying.

The chariots, examples of which have survived in Egyptian tombs (*e.g.*, the tomb of Tutankhamun), were light, springless, two-wheeled affairs. Each was occupied by two men, a driver and a warrior, the latter armed with bows, javelins, and a shield. In this the Egyptian chariotry resembled those described in the poems of Homer. The driver took a big risk, because he was not armed. His job was to maneuver the vehicle into the most advantageous position so that his comrade could shoot his arrows and hurl his spears. Two horses drew each chariot. The chariot force was split up into squadrons of twenty-five chariots apiece and there were also the "stable masters" responsible for the well-being of the horses. As the horseshoe had not yet been invented, there were no farriers.

The infantry were variously armed. Some were archers, who also carried axes and clubs. There were regiments of spearmen, armed with shields. Sometimes these spears were more than 6 feet long and may have been used as pikes were used in the Middle Ages: to present a hedge of points against a charge. There was also a *corps d'élite* of infantry known as the "Braves of the King," or simply "Braves." It was their duty to lead the attack. They stormed the breach in the ramparts of Kadesh when that city was taken by Tuthmosis III. Then there were special troops for garrison service, and the famous Medjay, who were desert police.

Transport was provided by asses, at least in the early part of the Eighteenth Dynasty. But Tuthmosis III introduced wagons drawn by oxen to transport boats for the crossing of the Euphrates, and afterwards oxcarts formed part of the equipment of the Egyptian Army.

By this time too, there was a complete hierarchy of military rank. There was a special name for privates which meant simply "members of the Army." The lowest grade of officer was the "greatest of fifty." Next came the "commander of a hundred" and above him the "standard-bearer." In Ramesside times (in the latter period of the New Empire) these standard-bearers commanded regiments of two hundred infantrymen. There were also names distinguishing volunteers from conscripts, for it seems to have been possible to make the Army a career, though propaganda against the military life was strong among the scribes (who were exempt from combat service).

Above the regimental commander came the "captain of a troop" and the "troop commander," who probably commanded a brigade of several regiments, and higher still in the military hierarchy came the "lieutenant commander of the Army." There were also administrative officers, such as the "Army scribe," the "scribe of the infantry," the "scribe of assemblage," and the "scribe of distribution."

We owe to one of these scribes perhaps the most impressive personal account which has come down to us of active service conditions in Syria. It dates from a slightly later period than that of Tuthmosis III, but the conditions described by Hori, the scribe in question, must have been exactly like those which Senmut and Kenamun encountered when they followed Menkheperre into Syria.

Hori was an official, evidently with great experience of Syrian campaigning, and his letter is addressed to one of his subordinates, Amenemope, a "scribe in command of the Army"—evidently an administrative officer responsible for food and supplies for the troops. Amenemope, it seems, had "fallen down on the job," and had tried to cover his incompetence by sending Hori a pompous letter in which he boasted of his prowess and attempted to display his knowledge of local conditions.

But every word of Hori's reply reveals the old veteran, seasoned in war, travel-wise and worldly; and yet behind the sardonic phrases with which he mocks his opponent there lurks, I suspect, a not unkind heart. I like to think of Hori sitting in his office in Thebes, his warfaring days over (and he is glad that they are over), yet remembering, not without relish his past: the days when he "commanded the auxiliary troops . . . the Shardana, the Kehek, the Mashawasha . . ." when he trod the road to Meger, "where the sky is dark by day, and . . . is overgrown with cypresses and oaks, and with cedars which reach Heaven," remembering Joppa, where he had found "a fair maiden that keepeth watch over the vineyards" . . . who "gave him the color of her bosom. . . ."

The following few fragments are from this vivid human document, as translated by Adolf Erman many years ago, which everyone who cares about Ancient Egypt should read in full in Erman's classic work, *The Literature of the Ancient Egyptians*.

One word of explanation before we begin. Amenemope has apparently described himself as a *mahir*—a word meaning "hero," and this has irritated the old veteran; he returns to it repeatedly in his satirical reply to his subordinate:

Thy letter aboundeth in thrusts, and is loaded with great words. Behold, they shall reward thee, even as thou look for a load, and shall lay more on thee than thou wouldst.

"I am a scribe, a *mahir*," thou sayest again. There is truth in thy words, say we. Come forth, that thou mayest be tested.

A horse is harnessed for thee, swift as a jackal . . . and it is like unto a storm of wind, when it goeth forth. Thou looseneth the reins (?) and seizeth the bow. We shall see what thine hand will do. I will expound to thee the nature of a *mahir*, and show thee what he doeth.

Hast thou not gone to the land of Khatti, and hast thou not seen the land of Upe? [2] Khedem—dost thou not know the nature of it, and Igedii too, what it is like? Sumur of Sesse—on which side of it lieth the town of Kher . . . ? What is its stream like? Hast thou not marched to Kadesh and Tubikhi? Hast thou not gone unto the region of the Bedouins with the auxiliary troops of the Army?

Hast thou not trodden the road to Meger, where the sky is dark by day, and it is overgrown with cypresses (?) and oaks, and with cedars that reach high heaven? There are more lions there than panthers and

[2] Locality near Damascus. A Canaanite name.

hyenas (?) and it is girt about with Bedouins on [every] side.

Hast thou not climbed Mount Shewe? Hast thou not trodden it, while thy hands are laid upon . . . and thy chariot is battered by the ropes as thy horse is dragged (?)?

Prithee let *me tell thee of* . . . beret. Thou shrinkest from climbing it and crossest [rather] its stream. . . . Thou beholdest how it tastes to be a *mahir*, when thou bearest thy chariot on thy shoulder. . . .

When thou comest to a halt in the evening, thy whole body is crushed . . . and thy limbs are broken. . . . Thou awakenest, when it is the hour for . . . in the . . . night.

Thou art alone to do the harnessing, brother cometh not to brother; the fugitives (?) have come into the camp, the horse hath been let loose, the . . . hath been ransacked (?) in the night, thy clothes have been stolen. Thy groom hath awakened in the night and hath marked *what they* (?) *have done;* he hath taken what was left, and hath joined (the ranks of) the wicked. He hath mingled with the tribes of the Bedouins and changed himself into an Asiatic. The foe came to pillage (?) in secret, and they found thee inert, and when thou didst awake thou didst find no trace of them, and they have made away with thy things. Thou art become a fully-equipped *mahir,* and takest hold of thine ear.[3]

[3] Probably a gesture of grief.

Then Hori challenges Amenemope to reveal his knowledge of Phoenicia (the modern Lebanon). Many of the towns he speaks of can still be identified—Berytus (modern Beirut), Tyre, and Byblos. I remember, during a recent visit to the Lebanon, reading this very passage on a hillside overlooking the ancient port of Byblos, looking down on the tangle of ruined walls, some of which may have been standing when Hori and his comrades knew them three thousand years ago.

I will tell thee of another mysterious city, Byblos by name. What is it like? Their goddess—of her another time. Hast thou not trodden it?

Come teach me about Berytus, and about Sidon and Sarepta. Where is the stream of Nezen, and what is Us like?

They say that another city lieth in the sea, whose name is Tyre of the Port (?). Water is taken unto it in boats (?) and it is richer in fish than in sand.[4]

I will tell thee of another misery—the crossing of Seram. Thou wilt say, "It burneth more than a sting." Very ill fares the *mahir*. . . .

Put me on the way to Hamath, to Deger, and to Deger-el, the playground of *mahirs*. Pray teach me about his road; show me Yan. If one is travelling to Edemem, whither turneth he the face? Turn not back from teaching [us?] and lead us (?) to them!

Later follows a wonderful passage on the crossing of Karmel, near Megiddo, which many conquerors have passed, from Tuthmosis III to General Allenby.

[4] The city of Tyre lay on a small rocky island.

Show me how to pass by Megiddo which lieth above it. Thou art a *mahir*, who is skilled in deeds of valour! A *mahir*, such as thou art, is qualified (?) to march (?) at the head of the host! Forward, O *maryen* [5] to shoot!

Behold there is (?) the . . . in a ravine (?) 2,000 cubits deep, filled with boulders and shingle. Thou makest a detour (?). Thou graspest the bow; thou . . . on thy left, thou lettest the chieftains see *what is pleasing to their eyes until thine hands groweth weary: "Abata Kemo ari, mahir naem."*

The latter are Canaanite words of which the approximate meaning, according to Erman, the translator, might be "Thou slayest like a lion, O pleasant *mahir*." Hori, of course, is also displaying his knowledge of the foreigners' language, just as a British 8th Army veteran might casually throw into his wartime reminiscences a few words of Arabic—or German.

Thou gainest the name of a . . . *mahir* [among the] officers of Egypt. Thy name becometh like that of Kazardi, the chief of Eser, when the hyena found him in the terebinth tree.

Behold, there is the narrow defile, made perilous by Bedouins, who are hidden beneath the bushes; some of them are of four cubits and five cubits from the nose unto the sole of the foot, fierce of face, their heart not mild, and they hearken not to coaxing.

Thou art alone, no helper is with thee, and no army is behind thee. Thou findest no guide to show

[5] Alternative to *mahir*.

thee a way of crossing. Thou determinest (?) to go forward, albeit thou knowest not the way. Shuddering (?) seizeth thee, the [hair of thy head] standeth on end, thy soul lieth in thine hand. Thy path is full of boulders and shingle, and there is *no passable track,* for it is overgrown with . . . thorns, *neh*-plants, and wolf's pad. The ravine is one side of thee, the mountain riseth on the other. On thou goest and guidest (?) thy chariot beside thee, and fearest to . . . thy horse. *If the horse falleth down* thine hand [6] falleth and is left bare, and thy . . . leather falleth. Thou unharnessest the horse, in order to repair the hand in the middle of the defile; thou art not expert in the way of binding it, and thou knowest not how to fasten it together (?) The . . . falleth from its place, and the horse is [already] too heavily [laden] to load him [with it]. Thou art sick at heart, and thou startest to go on foot. The sky is open, and thou fanciest that the enemy is behind thee. Then trembling taketh hold of thee. Ah, would that thou hadst a hedge of . . . that thou mightst put it upon the other side! Thy horse is galled up to the time that thou findest quarters for the night. Thou perceivest how pain tasteth.

Hori, now thoroughly warming to his subject, envisages the unhappy *mahir* surrendering to the charms of a Syrian girl and being subsequently detected and taken prisoner:

When thou enterest Joppa, thou findest the meadow growing green in its time [*i.e.,* when the

---

[6] "Hand" seems to mean a part of the chariot or its harness.

season is at its loveliest]. Thou forcest a way into . . .
and findeth the fair maiden that keepeth watch over
the vineyards. She taketh thee to herself as a companion and showeth thee the colour of her bosom.
Thou art recognised and bearest witness; the *mahir*
is put on trial, and thy tunic of good Upper Egyptian
linen, thou sellest it [as a bribe to facilitate his escape].
. . . Thou sleepest every evening, with a piece of
woollen cloth about thee, thou slumberest, and art
inert. Thy . . . thy bow, thy . . . knife, and thy
quiver are stolen, and thy reins are cut in the darkness.

Thine horse is gone and . . . over slippery
ground. The road stretchest out before it. It smashes
the chariot . . . thy weapons fall to the ground and
are buried in the sand. . . .

Then the *mahir* finds his way back to his Egyptian
comrades, but they do not recognize him, as he has lost his
clothes and equipment:

Thou beggest, "Give me food and water, for I
have arrived safely." They turn a deaf ear, they do
not listen, they pay no heed to thy tales.

Thou makest thy way into the smithy, and the
workshop surroundeth thee. Smiths and cobblers are
all about thee. They do all that thou wishest. They
attend to thy chariot, and it ceaseth to be slack. Thy
. . . are cut aright; its . . . are adjusted. They put
thy yoke to rights. . . . They give a . . . to thy
whip, and attach to it lashes. Forth thou goest to fight
on the field of battle, to accomplish deeds of valour. . . .

This last passage is, of course, purely ironical, since Amenemope is merely having his chariot put in order so that he can cut a good appearance when he returns to Egypt. And there we must leave him.

The document dates from the time of the second Rameses, and in after years it became a standard school exercise which the young scribes had to learn. The translation I have given is an old one, and Erman was forced to leave gaps in the place of many words, *e.g.*, those describing parts of the chariot, which he could not translate, and also to fill in gaps in the manuscript with conjectural readings (indicated by italics). But I know of no other passage in Ancient Egyptian literature which gives so convincing a picture of the life of a soldier under the Pharaohs of the Eighteenth Dynasty, more than three thousand years ago.

# CHAPTER 8

# PER-HOR GOES TO SCHOOL

THE greatest complex of buildings in Thebes, larger
even than the Royal Palace, is the Temple of Amun,
with its huge pylons, massive, sloping-sided, which
flank the ceremonial entrances; its towering hall of columns, beyond which lie the dark, mysterious chambers
where the most sacred rites are performed; the sunlit
courtyards across which walk the shaven white-robed
priest; the sky-pointing obelisks. All these are only the core
of what is almost a city within a city—a maze of corridors,
streets, storerooms, treasuries, granaries, and the domestic
quarters of the priests and priestesses who serve the King of
Gods. Among these buildings is a school, and in one of the
rooms which we enter now, twenty or so small boys sit
cross-legged on the floor.

At one end of the room sits their teacher, a venerable
scribe, a roll of papyrus spread out before him, and other
rolls at his side. Each boy has in front of him a piece of
potsherd, on which he is laboriously writing at the dictation
of the teacher. Later, when they become accomplished
scribes, they will be entrusted with papyrus, but for the
time being scraps of pottery are quite good enough. Later
these school exercises will be thrown away, to be unearthed
thousands of years later and pored over by scholars, whose
task of deciphering the ancient language will be made even

more difficult because of the schoolboys' grammatical mistakes.

One of the boys is Per-hor, the youngest son of Rekhmire. Like nearly all schoolboys of every generation, he does not like his lessons very much, and unlike his modern counterpart he has not even the possibility of gazing out of the window, for there are no windows in this room, only narrow apertures high in the mud-brick wall, through which the morning sunlight streams, throwing elongated patches of brightness on the ceiling. However, there are a few compensations; for instance, Khaemwese, the teacher, is old and rather deaf, so that one can, if one is careful, have quite interesting conversations with one's neighbor, varied occasionally with a game of marbles, the stones being concealed in Per-hor's tunic.

Care is necessary, however, for one of the maxims of the scribes, which Per-hor has had to copy out many times, is "The ear of a boy is on his back, and he harkeneth when he is beaten." And Khaemwese is no respecter of persons, even the son of the Vizier.

Per-hor is an intelligent lad, and most modern schoolboys would sympathize with his boredom, since the lessons consist chiefly of learning by rote, and laboriously copying out set exercises which have been used in Egyptian schools for generations.

Let us lean over his small shoulder and see what he has written:

> I place thee at school along with the children of notables, to educate thee and to have thee trained in this aggrandising calling.

Behold, I relate to thee how it fareth with the scribe when he . . . Wake up, at thy place, the books lie [already] before thy comrades. Place thine hand on thy clothes and look to thy sandals. When thou gettest thy daily task . . . be not idle. . . .

Per-hor's neighbor, young Nebamun, son of the Chief of the Granaries, is copying out another exercise:

I have heard that thou followest pleasures. Turn not thy back on my words. Dost thou give thy mind to all manner of deaf (?) things? . . .

I will cause thy foot to stumble when it goeth in the streets, and thou shalt be beaten with the hippo-patamus whip.

However, I have seen many like thee, that did sit in the writing academy and that said not "by God" without swearing, "Books are nothing at all." Yet they became scribes, and One [1] remembered their names, to despatch them on errands.

The pessimism of the Egyptian teacher regarding his pupils is bottomless. When Per-hor gets older, and becomes acquainted with pastimes less innocent than marbles, he will probably have to copy out the following exercise:

I am told that thou forsakest writing, thou givest thyself up (?) to pleasures; thou goest from street to street, where (?) it smelleth of beer, to destruction. Beer, it scareth men [from thee], it sendeth thy soul to perdition.

[1] Pharaoh.

Thou art like a broken steering-oar in a ship, that is obedient on neither side. Thou art like a shrine without its god, and like a house without bread.

Thou art encountered climbing a wall and breaking the . . . men run away from before thee, for thou inflictest wounds on them.

Would that thou knewest that wine is an abomination, that thou wouldst take an oath in respect of *shedeh*,[2] that thou shouldst not set thine heart on the bottle (?) and wouldst forget *telek*.[2]

Thou art taught to sing to the flute . . . and to pipe, to speak to the *kinnor* [3] in anen, and to sing to the *nezekh*.[3]

Thou sittest in the house [brothel?] and the girls encircle thee; thou standest and makest. . . .

Thou sittest in front of the wench and art besprinkled with oil; thy garland of *ishet-penu* hangeth about thy neck, and thou drummest on thy paunch.

Thou dost reel, and [then] fallest upon thy belly and art besmirched with dirt. . . .

Most of the lessons which have survived are admonitory, but whatever the context the scribe never fails to praise his own calling, and to denigrate those of others. To judge from Egyptian school literature the student was subjected to an almost continuous barrage of propaganda on behalf of the craft of letters. In Ancient Egypt the lettered man was an educated man; only by learning the art of

[2] Intoxicating drinks.
[3] Foreign musical instruments.

1. The pyramid plateau from Abusir, looking north towards Giza pyramids.

2. Boats on the Nile at Luxor.

3. The Goddess Isis suckling the infant Horus.

4. In a royal tomb in the Valley of the Tombs of the Kings, Rameses II *(left)* offering to the God Horus *(hawk-headed)*.

5. Rekhmire's boat (from his tomb).

6. Cattle boats on the Nile (from a tomb painting).

7. Step Pyramid of Djoser at Sakkara.

8. Step Pyramid at Sakkara in late afternoon. The Pyramid is the oldest large stone-built monument in the world, built by Imhotep, chief architect of King Djoser (2800 B.C.).

9.  A great estate of the Eighteenth Dynasty.

10. Child's chair from the tomb of Tutankhamun.

11. A "soul house" (Twelfth Dynasty).

12. Another example of a "soul house" (notice the stairs leading to the upper apartments).

13. From the tomb of the Vizier Nakht in the Theban Necropolis. Dancing girls performing at a banquet given by the Vizier. Three male guests (with lotus flowers) at top left-hand corner.

14. Guests at a banquet (Eighteenth Dynasty). *Top:* Male and female guests served by handmaidens. *Bottom:* Girl dancers and musicians. Wine jars on right.

15. (*Above*) Group of Ancient
Egyptian musical instruments
—two harps, a castanet in the
shape of an arm, and a pipe.

16. (*Right*) Painted figure of
a girl playing a harp.

17. Tomb of Khereuf in the Theban Necropolis. The young daughters of
Amenophis III walking in procession.

18. The wife of the Vizier Nakht, an Eighteenth Dynasty nobleman, from his tomb in the Theban Necropolis.

19. *(Below)* A group of women's toilet articles — casket, spoon for mixing eye paint, comb, cosmetic jar and bronze mirror.

20. Female portrait bust in the Cairo Museum.

21. Artist's sketch of a woman suckling a child.

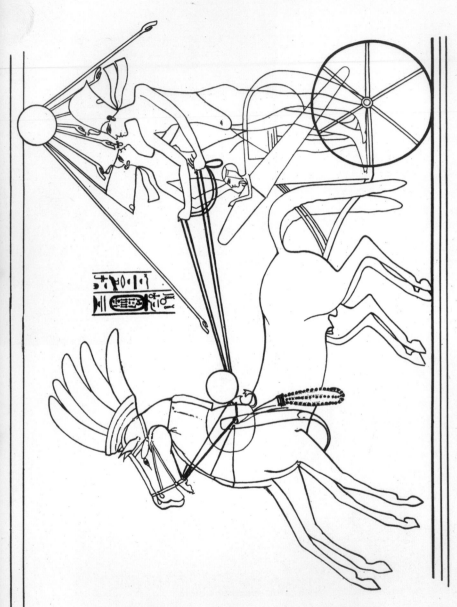

22. Nefretiti and Akhenaten in chariot with their small daughter. From a tomb at Tell-el-Amarna.

23. Tomb fresco showing a nobleman catching wild fowl while his wife (*right*) watches.

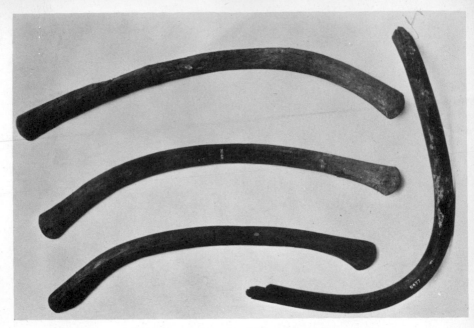

24. Boomerangs used for wild-fowling.

25. Young Egyptian girl.

26. Temple of Karnak: scene from the annual procession in honor of the God Amun. Frieze of Egyptian warriors with shields.

27. The gold-encased chariot of Tutankhamun.

28. Egyptian infantry on the march (a Twelfth Dynasty model).

29. Wooden toy horse.

30. Toy lion with movable jaw.

51

[15671]
WOODEN TOY
LION WITH MOVEABLE LOWER JAW
[Roman period]

31. Spinning tops.

32. Balls of painted fabric.

33. Example of "hieratic" script.

34. Scribe's palette.

35. Metalworkers and carpenters (from the tomb of Rekhmire). This picture merits study. Notice the use of the drill (*top*), sawing and chopping of wood, furnace with foot-operated bellows (*bottom*) and pouring of molten metal into molds (*bottom right*).

36. Craftsmen in the Temple of Amun (from the tomb of Rekhmire).

37. Men making statues (from the tomb of Rekhmire).

38. Alabaster vases of the Third Dynasty (2800 B.C.) found under the Step Pyramid of Djoser.

39. Groups of carpenters' tools. The small objects *(bottom left)* are drills which are rotated by a bow *(near center)*.

40. Granite block showing method of splitting. The Egyptians first chiseled holes in the stone. Wooden wedges were then driven into the holes and soaked in water. The expansion of the wood split the rock.

41. Gold portrait mask of Tutankhamun.

42. Relief from the Temple of Karnak depicting the annual procession in the honor of the God Amun. Dancing girls performing a ritual dance followed by women shaking the *sistra*.

43. Mummy of Tuthmosis III
(the Napoleon of Ancient
Egypt), greatest king of the
Eighteenth Dynasty (circa
1500 B.C.). Compare statue
below.

44. Statue of Tuthmosis III.

45. Fresco of the Young Prince. (An example of the Cretans, from the Palace of Knossos in Crete. These may have been the *Keftiu.*)

46. The Theban Necropolis, looking west from the Rest House.

47. Tomb fresco from the tomb of Rekhmire. Rekhmire and wife receiving offerings from his children.

48. Keftiu and Nubians bringing tribute.

49. The Nile at Luxor, looking westwards to the Theban hills (in which lies the Necropolis).

50. The funerary temple of Queen Hatshepsut at Deir-el-Bahri (near Thebes).

51. Colossal statues of Amenophis III in his temple at Luxor.

writing could a young man qualify for what in modern terms would be called a "Government job."

Beside old Khaemwese, who sits with his eyes half closed as his pupils write, lies a pile of papyrus rolls, exercises which he himself probably had to practice when he was a boy, and which he has given to generations of pupils. Let us look at some of them.

Here is one warning the pupil against becoming a soldier:

Ah, what meanest thou by saying, "It is thought that the soldier is better off than the scribe"?

Come let me tell thee how the soldier fareth, the oft-belaboured, when he is brought while yet a . . . child, to be shut up in the barracks (?). He receiveth a burning (?) blow on his body, a ruinous blow on his eye, a blow layeth him out on his eyebrow, and his pate is cleft with a wound. He is laid down and beaten, like a document. He is battered and bruised with flogging.

Come, let me tell thee how he goeth to Syria, and how he marcheth over the mountains. His bread and water are borne upon his shoulder like the load of an ass; they make his neck as . . . that of an ass, and the joints of his back are bowed. His drink is stinking water. When he reacheth the enemy, he is like a trapped (?) bird, and he hath no strength in his limbs.

If he cometh back home to Egypt, he is like wood that the worm eateth. He is sick and becometh bedridden. He is brought back upon an ass; his clothes are stolen, and his servant hath run away.

O scribe Ennana, turn thee away from the thought that the soldier is better off than the scribe. . . .

But, objects the pupil, that may be true of the common soldier, but an officer fares better surely? To be an officer of chariotry, *that* would be a good life! But the teacher has him there, too, and grimly hands out another lesson. Per-hor, as he copies out this one, makes a mental note to pass on its contents to his elder brother, Kenamun:

Set thy heart on being a scribe, that thou mayest direct the whole earth.

Come, let me tell thee of a miserable calling, that of the officer of chariotry. He is placed in the stable because of the father of his mother [out of regard for his good family] with five slaves; two men of them are given him as helpers.

He hasteneth to get steeds from the stall in his majesty's presence. When he hath obtained goodly horses, he is glad and exulteth. [*Like a modern young man with a new sports car—L.C.*] He cometh with them into town, and he trampleth it underfoot with zest. Happy is he when he thus trampleth underfoot . . . [but] he knoweth not [yet] how it is with him.

He expendeth his wealth which he hath from the father of his mother, that he may acquire a chariot. Its pole costeth three *deben* and the chariot costs five *deben*.

He hasteneth to trample underfoot from upon it. He maketh himself into one that is shod . . . he taketh himself and thrusteth himself into the sandals. He casteth the chariot away in the thicket, and his feet are cut by the sandals, and his shirt is pierced with thorns.

When one cometh to muster the troops (?) he is grievously beaten; he is beaten upon the ground, beaten with a hundred stripes.

And once again comes the unvarying refrain:

Be a scribe, who is freed from forced labour, and protected from all work.

The bewildered youth thinks that perhaps a farmer's life would offer compensations. But would it?

Dost thou not bethink thee how it fareth with the husbandman, when the harvest is registered. The worm hath taken half the corn, the hippopotamus hath devoured the rest.[4] The mice abound in the field, and the locust hath descended. The cattle devour, and the sparrows steal. Woe to the husbandman!

The remainder, that lieth upon the threshing-floor, the thieves make an end of that. The . . . of copper is destroyed; the pair of horses dieth at the threshing and ploughing.

And now the scribe landeth on the embankment and will register the harvest. The porters carry sticks, and the Negroes palm-ribs. They say, "Give corn."

[4] Compare the American folk song, "The Boll Weevil": "The tax man got half the cotton, the boll weevil got the rest. . . ."

"There is none here."

He is stretched out and beaten; he is bound and thrown into the canal. His wife is bound in his presence, his children are put in fetters (?). His neighbours leave them, they take to flight, and look after their corn.

But the scribe, he directeth the work of all people. For him there are no taxes, for he payeth tribute in writing, and there are no dues for him. Prithee, know that.

Even the priest is not exempt from forced labor:

The priest standeth there as an husbandman, and the *we'eb*-priest worketh in the canal. . . .

The baker is even more unfortunate:

When the baker standeth and baketh and layeth bread on the fire, his head is inside the oven, and his son holdeth fast his feet. Cometh it to pass that he slippeth from his son's hand, he falleth into the blaze. But the scribe, he directeth every work that is in this land.

Poor Per-hor! Did he and his schoolfellows believe all this? Not all of them presumably, since there was never any lack of soldiers, farmers, craftsmen, priests, and tradesmen in Ancient Egypt. But it was true that for any young man who wished to rise to high administrative rank it was necessary to master the difficult art of writing. Just how difficult it was can be discovered by any reader who cares to consult a primer of the ancient language and take the first few steps towards learning it. If he gives up in despair (as I did), he will at least come away with an increased respect for the boys who learned it in ancient times, and even more for the modern scholars who, at a distance of five thousand years, have given us the translations from which I have drawn so liberally for this book.

For it was not an easy language to learn. It began as a system of picture-writing, which served well enough to recall something to the writer's mind, but from which a reader would have difficulty in discovering the desired idea. For instance, to quote from Erman's introduction to his admirable *Literature of the Ancient Egyptians:*

. . . If two people agree that the one is to supply an ox in three months' time, in return for which the other will pay five jars of honey, pictures of the moon, the ox, the bee, and the jar, in addition to small strokes indicating the numbers, suffice as tokens for them both, but a third person would never be able to explain these signs with certainty. This preliminary structure must therefore undergo considerable development. Individual peoples have proceeded on very different lines, and have thereby arrived at all sorts of writing of words and syllables. The Egyptians alone were destined to adopt a remarkable method, following which they attained to the highest form of writing, the alphabet.

Fundamentally the method was quite simple. As the system of writing developed and the Egyptian wanted to write words which it would have been difficult, or even impossible, to draw (because of the number and complexity of the symbols), he began to substitute for such words other words, which could be easily drawn, *and which had a similar sound*. From the context the reader would recognize what was really meant. For instance, the hieroglyphic sign (➣) , the swallow, had the sound *wr*. But the sound *wr* also meant "great"; the reader could easily tell which meaning was intended. Or take the sign (🪲) , the beetle, which had the sound *khpr*. The same sound also meant "to become." To quote Erman again:

> Since in Egyptian, as in the related languages, the meaning of a word is attached to its consonants, whereas the vowels decide its grammatical form, regard was only paid to the fact that the word which had been substituted for another had the same consonants as it, while the vowels were disregarded. It was if—to take an English example—"heed" were written with the picture of a "head" and "broad" with that of a loaf of "bread."

This explains why Ancient Egyptian presents such brain-racking problems to the modern translator. The Ancient Egyptian, knowing the missing vowel sounds, would know, for instance, whether the word *szm* meant "to hear," "hears," "is heard," "may hear," "hearing," or "heard."

It is this lack of vowel sounds which makes translation so difficult. The Ancient Egyptian reader would know at a glance whether the *szm* in question was pronounced *sazem* or *sizam* or *sezum*, and the precise meaning attached to each. This causes philologists many headaches, and explains why they often disagree on the meaning of Egyptian words. It also explains why, if you picked up a learned periodical, such as the *Journal of Egyptian Archaeology*, you may be arrested by a four-thousand-word article with the fascinating title, "A Special Use of the *sdm.f* and *sdm.n.f.* Forms" —and then pass on hurriedly to "The Report on the Slave-girl Senbet."

So when you read translations of Ancient Egyptian texts, do not be irritated by those mysterious gaps in the middle of a particularly interesting passage. It may be that part of the manuscript is missing, or that, after trying hard to arrive at the meaning, the translator has had to give up rather than commit himself to a doubtful reading. Also do not be surprised if, when comparing two translations of the same passage, different meanings are given to the same words. Progress in decipherment is slow but continuous, and many of the translations which appear in earlier works on Egypt are now partly outdated. For instance, a scholar such as Sir Alan Gardiner or Professor Fairman might give a somewhat different rendering of the passages I have quoted in Erman's translation.

To return to the development of the language: a time came when such simple signs as I have mentioned were transferred to so many words that they were hardly ever used for special ones; they became *phonetic* signs. Thus, says Erman, "the swallow is used not only, as in the first instance, for *wr,* 'great,' but also to write the consonants *w* and *r* in words like *hwr, swr, wrs, wrryt,* etc."

Other peoples had arrived at this stage in the development of their language, but the Egyptians went even further.

Using as consonants the signs for short words containing only one consonant, they eventually arrived at an alphabet of twenty-four consonants. And here we come to a difficult point. Erman believed that the Phoenicians, from whom the Greeks borrowed their alphabet, derived theirs in turn from the Ancient Egyptians. A great many scholars believe this too, notably Sir Alan Gardiner. More than thirty years ago, Sir Alan, with Professor Peet, was entrusted with the publication of certain inscriptions discovered and copied by Sir Flinders Petrie at Serabit el-Khadim in central Sinai. Among these were copies of ten rock tablets, some of which, in Sir Alan's words, "were clearly borrowed from the hieroglyphs, whilst others were equally clearly not so borrowed." Among these non-Egyptian signs the scholar noticed an oxhead. Sir Alan says:

> This brought to mind the old contention of Gesenius that the prototypes of the Phoenician letters must originally have had the shapes indicated by the Hebrew letter names, and accordingly I exclaimed to my companion, "Surely we must here have the origin of the Phoenician *âleph.*"

He persisted, and

. . . to my astonishment, almost perfect equivalents were found for *bêth*, "house," *mêm*, "water"—the Egyptians always depicted water as a zigzag line— *ayin*, "eye," and *rêsh*, "head," besides others for one reason or another less convincing. . . .

The total number of different signs did not exceed thirty-two, "and of these some might well be variants; the natural inference was that the writing was alphabetic."

Then Sir Alan isolated a sequence of letters in this hitherto unknown script which occurred no less than six times. Applying his principle, he read the first sign as *B*, the second as ' (*'ayin*)—a peculiar guttural sound not heard in English—and the last as *T*. The third sign puzzled him for a while.

Running my eye down the Phoenician alphabet in the first reference book which came to hand, I naturally stopped at *lamedh* [a diagonal line with a hook at the bottom].

There was a similar line in the Sinaitic inscription, but in this case the hook was at the top. But if it was the same sign, then the meaning should be *L*. Putting the four consonants together, Sir Alan read the word *Ba'alat*.

Ba'alat was the Phoenician goddess, consort of Baal.

The regular Egyptian translation of the Semitic divine name Ba'alat was Hathor (so at Byblus) and . . . the goddess of the temple of Serabit [where the tablets were found] was well known to be "Hathor, lady of the Turquoise," her name occurring on a large majority of the hieroglyphic inscriptions there found. . . . Could this be mere coincidence? I thought and still think not. But if not, I had hit upon the origin of the alphabet, for the train of reasoning employed formed a rigid system, and if the conclusion were accepted, it would be wellnigh impossible to deny the premises. In other words, but for an almost unbelievable chance, the name Ba'alat is the true reading and demonstrates a genetic relationship between the Egyptian hieroglyphs, the Sinai characters, and the Phoenician letters with their traditional names.

I have digressed slightly to tell this story, because it illustrates the sudden drama which can sometimes illuminate a life devoted to patient, unexciting research. Also, if Sir Alan's conclusions are correct, and many scholars support him, then the characters in which this book is written owe their ultimate origin, not to Phoenicia, but to the Ancient Egyptians. From them they passed, via Palestine, to Phoenicia, and thence through the Greeks and the Romans to us.

So maybe we are linked, be it ever so tenuously, with little Per-hor, as he squats cross-legged in his classroom, longing for the lesson to end, while his tired hand laboriously copies out the words:

Fortunate is a scribe that is skilled in his calling, a master of education. Persevere every day; thus shalt

thou obtain the mastery over it. . . . Spend no day in
idleness, or thou wilt be beaten. The ear of a boy is on
his back, and he harkeneth when he is beaten. . . .

Suddenly old Khaemwese rises, and begins to gather
up his manuscripts. There is a stir in the class, which is instantly silenced by the master. Then the small boys stand
up, and, led by Khaemwese, say a prayer to Amun in sing-
song voices. Then, still under the stern eye of the old man,
they file quietly out into the sunlight, but the moment they
get outside, there is a babel of voices. The boys break
up into laughing groups. A couple are struggling on the
ground, rolling in the dust; others have produced a ball
which they toss to each other. Per-hor and Nebamun are
racing madly along the sunlit street towards the great
gate, heedless of the warning shouts of passing priests.
They reach the gate, and there, to the surprise and delight of Per-hor, waits his elder brother Kenamun, standing in a brand-new chariot and trying to look nonchalant.
The little boys gather round, loudly admiring the two sleek
horses with their nodding plumes, and the gold mountings
of the vehicle which gleam in the sun.

Per-hor is in his seventh heaven. He is proud of his big
brother, proud to know that he has been appointed an
officer of chariotry, proud to tell his friends that Kenamun
is shortly to follow His Majesty to the land of the Mountain-dwellers. Nonetheless, he is just as capable of mischief
as other small boys, and as Kenamun proudly drives through
the streets of Thebes, with Per-hor hanging on grimly to
the rail, the youngster recalls one of the exercises which he
has had to copy out that morning.

And so, above the clopping of the hoofs and the noise of the streets, he begins to recite in a loud voice:

"Come, let me tell thee of a miserable calling, that of the officer of chariotry. . . ."

"What's that?" asks Kenamun.
The small voice goes on relentlessly:

"He hasteneth to get steeds from the stall in his majesty's presence. When he hath obtained goodly horses, he is glad and exulteth. . . ."

Kenamun tries to box his brother's ears, but Per-hor ducks. Standing as far as possible from Kenamun, and dancing up and down with delight, he shouts:

"He cometh with them into town, and he trampleth it underfoot with zest. Happy is he when he thus trampleth underfoot, [but] he knoweth not [yet] how it is with him. . . ."

Now they are nearing Rekhmire's house. Kenamun has his hands full with the mettlesome horses, to which he is still not accustomed, so Per-hor is free to continue his mockery:

"He maketh himself into one that is shod. . . . He casteth the chariot away in the thicket. . . . When One cometh to muster the troops (?) he is grievously tormented; he is beaten upon the ground, beaten with a hundred stripes."

The chariot draws up at the porter's lodge and grooms hasten out to take the horses. Kenamun, laughing, tries to grab his brother, but the boy is too quick for him. At the top of the steps he stands for a moment, jigging up and down and calling out, "Be a scribe! Be a scribe!"

The Nubian porter and the grooms are smiling. With a final taunt of "Be a scribe!" Per-hor takes to his heels. As he races up the path to the house, Kenamun picks up a piece of earth and flings it after the retreating figure. But he misses.

# CHAPTER 9

# THE CRAFT OF WRITING

THE Egyptians were a practical people. Their great achievements in architecture and sculpture, in astronomy and mathematics, had originally a purely utilitarian purpose. Unlike the Greeks, who admired them greatly, they seem to have had little intellectual curiosity, no love of knowledge for its own sake. Abstract speculation held no interest for them. And yet the Greeks owed the Egyptians a great deal—as they freely acknowledged. Thales, for example, was impressed and stimulated by Egyptian civilization. What the Greeks found in Egypt was an immense fund of useful practical knowledge, not exactly science as we understand the word, but at any rate, the raw material of science.

To take one example, mathematics, in which the Greeks excelled, R. W. Sloley in *The Legacy of Egypt* writes:

> The Egyptian developed a practical system of numeration and could carry out arithmetical calculations (involving the manipulation of complicated fractional expressions) with ease and accuracy. . . . He could solve problems involving two unknown quantities and had elementary notions of arithmetical progression using fractions, as well as of geometrical

progression. He was familiar with the elementary properties of rectangles, circles, and pyramids. Thus he could deal successfully with mathematical problems encountered in his daily life. The examples we have throw light on the methods of trading, the feeding of livestock, the raising of taxes, and the determination of values of food and drink in terms of the amount which can be made from a given quantity of material.

. . . Most of the problems deal with the concrete —seven loaves, five men—rarely with abstract numbers. While the Egyptian knew how to deal with particular cases, there is little evidence that he realised the underlying principles. The examples [given in the "Mathematical Papyri"] employ, for the most part, simple numbers and must be regarded as illustrations of method, model solutions, easy to learn by heart and apply to other similar problems.

The same thread of practicality runs through their achievements in art. The masterpieces of sculpture which astonish us were not created and enjoyed for their own sake. Many of them were never intended to be seen by human eyes. Some were realistic representations of the dead, placed in the tomb chambers and often hidden from sight, as dwelling places for the *ka* or spirit. Again, the lovely sculptured or painted frescoes which delight us in the tomb chapels, scenes which illustrate so vividly and charmingly the daily life of the Ancient Egyptians, were not put there for decorative purposes, nor primarily to advertise the wealth and importance of the deceased. Their purpose was magical, to insure that they had in the after-life all the possessions and amenities they enjoyed in this one. The soldier would have his troops, the country gentle-man his farms and estates and an endless supply of food offerings, even if their descendants failed to make actual offerings at the tomb. The painted or sculptured representa-tion became, by sympathetic magic, the real thing.

Writing began in a similar down-to-earth way. It was a working tool, a means by which a man could communi-cate with others without having to meet and talk with them, a means of keeping records and accounts, of record-ing events, and of writing down religious texts which, be-ing made permanent, perpetuated their magical powers. Hieroglyphic writing was already well developed at the time of the first recorded Egyptian dynasty, about 3200 B.C. The earliest examples of these signs are found en-graved or painted on stone vessels or other objects. Hiero-glyphic symbols were particularly well adapted for this purpose, since they can be arranged to be read from right to left, from left to right, or even vertically, according to the requirements of the decorative pattern. Throughout the three thousand years of Egyptian history the hiero-glyphic script was employed for all religious purposes, such as for inscriptions on the walls of temples and tombs, and for monumental inscriptions of all kinds. But for everyday purposes they were too elaborate; the ordinary Egyptian felt just as we would feel if we were asked to write all our correspondence in capital letters—and the hieroglyphs were much more complicated. So he developed a quicker, ab-breviated script which the Greeks called "hieratic," a kind of "running hand." The language was exactly the same, but the symbols were easier to write.

Most of the documents I have quoted in this book were written in hieratic on papyrus (see illustration on Plate 33). The early invention of this writing material also helped to develop the Egyptian written language. Unlike the Babylonians, who had to use baked clay as a writing material, the Egyptians had at hand unlimited supplies of papyrus reeds, which grew in abundance on the fringes of the Nile. The stem of the plant was first stripped of its outermost layer and cut into long strips. These were placed side by side and other strips laid across them at right angles. Then the two layers were placed together and the whole sheet dried and pressed. In this way it was possible to make "books," or rolls, of any length; manuscripts exist which are over one hundred feet in length. In later times papyrus scrolls were exported to other parts of the ancient world— for example, to Greece. In fact, we owe to Ancient Egypt the preservation of Greek literature, since "the vehicle by which Greek literature was preserved and transmitted from earliest times until perhaps the second or third century after Christ was the papyrus roll" (*Cambridge Companion to Greek Studies*).

Very early in Egyptian history the craft of writing, originally developed for purposes of utility, developed into an art. For the Egyptians, like all civilized and articulate peoples, discovered that words have a magic of their own, so in time there arose poets, and writers of stories and romances, who used language for no other purpose than to give pleasure.

As I have already quoted several examples of Egyptian lyric poetry (mainly of the New Empire) in the earlier part of this book, I shall devote the rest of this chapter to a few examples of the prose literature.

Long before the invention of writing, there probably existed poetry and folk tales which were recited and transmitted orally, as were the epic poems from which eventually grew the *Iliad* and the *Odyssey* of Homer. But if the pre-Dynastic Egyptians had any epic poetry it has not survived. There are, however, a number of fairy stories, fantastic tales of magical adventure which later scribes wrote down, and which may have roots in the childhood of the race. Judging from the surviving literature, the Egyptian seems to have loved stories of magicians and miraculous happenings. Except in the straightforward and usually dull biographies of officials, or the chronicles of kings and princes, there is little realism in early Egyptian literature. The more fantastic and improbable a story was, the better the Ancient Egyptian liked it. Perhaps this was an unconscious revolt against the restricted, overregulated lives which most of them were forced to lead.

One of the earliest of the magical tales is "King Cheops and the Magicians." Cheops, of course, was the builder of the Great Pyramid in about 2500 B.C., and the tale is a very ancient one, though the manuscript from which Erman made this translation dates only from the Hyksos period, one thousand years later. It is a naïve, popular tale, such as may well have been recited in the streets by public storytellers.

King Cheops asks his sons to tell him stories of the great magicians of the past. First Prince Chephren (builder of the Second Pyramid) tells him of a wondrous happening in the time of King Nebka, one of his predecessors. There was a certain *kherheb* (magician) named Ubaoner, who had an unfaithful wife. Suspecting that she was having an *affaire* with a townsman, who passed the time with her "in the pleasure-house in the lake of Ubaoner," the magician made a waxen crocodile, "seven spans long," and said to his house steward, "When the townsman goeth down into the lake according to his daily wont, then do thou throw the crocodile into the water behind him."

So the house-steward went his way and took the waxen crocodile with him.

And the wife of Ubaoner sent unto the house-steward that was in charge of the lake, saying "Let the pleasure-house which is in the lake be furnished. Lo, I come to dwell therein." And the pleasure-house was furnished with every good thing. Then they [1] went and spent a mirthful day with the townsman.

Now when it was evening, the townsman came according to his daily wont. And the house-steward threw the waxen crocodile behind him into the water, and it became a crocodile of seven cubits, and it laid hold on the townsman. . . . But Ubaoner tarried for seven days with the Majesty of the King Nebka, *and meanwhile the townsman was in the water without* breathing. Now, when the seven days were passed, King Nebka came . . . and the chief *kherheb*, Ubaoner, *presented himself before him.* And Ubaoner said: . . . "May thy majesty come and view the won-

[1] The wife and her maid.

der that hath come to pass in the time of thy majesty."
*The king went with him, and Ubaoner called the
crocodile and said,* "Bring thou hither the townsman." Then the crocodile came forth *and brought
him.* . . . And the majesty of King Nebka said:
"Your pardon, but this crocodile is frightful (?)."
Thereupon Ubaoner stooped down and took it, and it
became a waxen crocodile in his hand. . . .

Later Prince Baufre rises to speak, and tells Cheops of
"a wonder that came to pass in the time of thy father,
Snofru, one of the deeds of the chief *kherheb,* Zazamonkh."
The tale begins with the bored King seeking a diver-
sion. He assembles the officers of the palace and asks for sug-
gestions, but none satisfy him. Finally, he calls for the
magician Zazamonkh, who says to him:

"If Thy Majesty would but betake thee to the
lake of the Great House! Man thee a boat with all fair
damsels of the inner apartments of thy palace. Then
will the heart of Thy Majesty be diverted, when thou
shalt see how they row to and fro. Then, thou viewest
the pleasant nesting-places of thy lake, and viewest its
fields and pleasant banks, thine heart will be diverted
thereby."

The King thinks this is a good idea, but decides to improve on it.

*His Majesty said unto him:* "I *will do this: get
thee back to thine house* (?) but I will go boating.

THE CRAFT OF WRITING

Have brought to me twenty paddles of ebony in-wrought with gold. Have brought to me twenty women, of those with the fairest limbs, and with [beauteous] breasts and braided tresses, such as have not yet given birth, and moreover have brought me twenty nets, and to give these nets to these women instead of their clothes." And it was done according to all that His Majesty commanded. And they rowed to and fro, and the heart of His Majesty was glad when he beheld how they rowed.

Then a leader became entangled (?) with her braided tresses, and a fish-pendant [2] of new malachite fell into the water. And she became silent and ceased rowing, and her side [the girls on her side of the boat] became silent and ceased rowing. Then said His Majesty, . . . "Wherefore rowest thou not?" She said: "It is the fish-pendant of new malachite that hath fallen into the water." He had *another brought to her* and said: "I give thee this instead." And she said: "I want my pot down to its bottom." [3] Then said His Majesty: "Go to, and bring me the chief *kher-heb*, Zazamonkh." And he was brought straight-way.

The King then explains the position, whereupon the obliging magician performs, in miniature, the same act which Moses was to accomplish much later at the crossing of the Red Sea.

[2] A hair ornament. She probably entangled her hair with her paddle.
[3] Doubtless a proverb: "I want my right in full, my own thing" (Erman).

Then the chief *kherheb* Zazamonkh said his say of magic, and he placed the one side of the water of the lake upon the other, and found the fish-pendant lying on a potsherd. And he brought it and gave it to his mistress. Now as for the water, it was twelve cubits deep in the middle, and it reached twenty-four cubits after it was turned back [in other words, Zazamonkh folded the water back like a cloth]. Then he said his say of magic, and he brought the waters of the lake back to their place.

This is only a fragment of the full story, but it will suffice to show the charming, unsophisticated character of these popular tales. To me they suggest an odd mixture of *The Thousand and One Nights* and Boccaccio.

As a contrast, I am going to quote fairly fully from my favorite among all Egyptian stories, "The Story of Sinuhe." This dates from the Twelfth Dynasty, a period of intense literary sophistication, when "metaphor runs riot, and decadent features like a deliberate preciosity are not wanting. One Twelfth Dynasty writer pathetically complains of the difficulty of finding anything new to say, in fact there is abundant evidence that literature was now an art supremely conscious of itself" (Gardiner).

But there is nothing precious in the telling of this story; nor are there any magical happenings. This is the work of an accomplished literary craftsman who knows how to tell a story with economy and pace, how to delineate character, how to paint a scene, to describe action, to evoke pathos. It reads like a true story, which it may be.

But whether a piece of history or a work of fiction, it stands on its own feet as a piece of writing.

Sinuhe was a "prince and count" under the great King of the Twelfth Dynasty, Amenemhat I. While accompanying the King's son, Sesostris, on a punitive expedition against the Libyans west of the Delta, news is brought that the old King has died. For some reason which he never adequately explains, Sinuhe is aghast at the news, either because he fears that civil war will break out or because he believes that there is a plot to turn the young King against him. Whatever the reason, he decides to fly. The translation is Erman's.

In the year 30, on the ninth day of the third month of the Inundation, the god entered his horizon. King Amenemhat flew away to Heaven and was united with the sun, and the god's body was merged with his creator. The Residence was hushed, hearts were filled with mourning, the Two Great Portals were shut, the courtiers sat head on knees, and the people grieved.

Now, His Majesty had sent forth an army to the land of Temehu, and his eldest son was captain thereof, the god Sesostris; and even now he was returning, having carried away captives of the Tehenu and all manner of cattle without count.

And the Chamberlains of the Royal Palace sent to the western border [of the Delta] to inform the King's son of the event that had befallen at Court. And the messengers met him on the road and reached him at eventide. Not a moment did he tarry; the hawk flew away with his henchmen,[4] and did not make it known unto his army. Howbeit, a message had been sent unto the King's children that were with him in this army, and one of them had been summoned. And lo, I stood and heard his voice as he spake, being a little way [off].

Then was mine heart distraught. Mine arms sank, and trembling fell on all my limbs. I betook me thence leaping, to seek me a hiding-place. I placed me between two bushes so as to sunder the road from its traveller.

I set out southward, yet did not purpose to reach the Residence [*i.e.*, the Palace], for I thought that strife would arise, and I was not minded to live after him. I crossed the waters of Maaty, hard by the Sycamore, and came to the island of Snefru, and tarried there in a plot of ground. I was afoot early, and when it was day I met a man who stood in my path; he shrank from me and was afraid. The time of the evening meal came, and I drew nigh unto Ox-town. I crossed over in a barge without a rudder, with the aid of the breath of the west wind, and passed on east of the quarry, in the region of the Mistress of the Red Mountain.

Anyone who knows Egypt north of Cairo will be able roughly to follow the route taken by the fugitive Count. He fled from the army on the west bank of the Nile, followed the river southward to the place where it does not yet branch apart, and there crossed it "in a barge without a

[4] *I.e.*, the Prince left immediately with his followers.

rudder." Then he must have passed near the site of modern Cairo, for the "Red Mountain," still so called, is near Cairo, and the quarries are still worked. From this place Sinuhe struck northeastward towards the frontier, intending to make his escape into Palestine.

I gave a road to my feet northwards, and attained the Wall of the Prince [a frontier fortress], which was made to repel the Asiatics. I bowed me down in a thicket lest the watcher for the day on the wall should espy me.

He approaches the Isthmus of Suez, passing through arid desert.

At eventide I passed on, and when day dawned I reached Peten and halted on the island of Kemwer. There it o'ertook me that I fell down for thirst, I was parched, my throat burned, and I said, "This is the taste of death." Then I lifted up mine heart, for I heard the lowing of cattle and descried Bedouins. The sheikh among them, who had been in Egypt, recognised me. He gave me water, and cooked milk for me, and I went with him to his tribe, and they treated me kindly.

Sinuhe continues his journey towards Syria, the "land of Retenu," as the Egyptians called it. The writer does not bother to describe the countries passed through, mentioning only the famous Phoenician port of Byblos, which most Egyptians would know by name.

Land gave me to land. I set forth from Byblos and drew near to Kedemi and spent half a year there. Nenshi, the son of Amu, the Prince of Upper Retenu, took me and said unto me, "Thou farest well with me, for thou hearest the speech of Egypt." This said he, for he had become aware of my qualities, and had heard of my wisdom; Egyptians that dwelt with him had testified to him concerning me.

He said to me, "Why art thou come hither? Hath aught befallen at the Residence?" And I said to him, "King Sehetepibre hath gone to the Horizon, and none knoweth what hath happened in the matter." And I said again, dissembling: "I came from the expedition to the land of the Temehu, and report was made unto me, and mine heart trembled and mine heart was no longer in my body. It carried me away upon the pathways of the wastes. Yet none hath gossiped about me, none hath spat in my face; I had heard no reviling word, and my name hadn't been heard in the mouth of the herald. I know not what brought me to this land. It was like the dispensation of God."

It seems that Sinuhe had reconciled himself to a long period of exile, for he accepts Nenshi's invitation to settle in his land. So the exiled Egyptian nobleman adopts the manners and customs of the Asiatics, who to him are, of course, barbarians. He marries Nenshi's eldest daughter and has children by her. The Chief of the Northern Retenu gives him land and places him in authority over his bravest tribe. And Sinuhe serves Nenshi faithfully in peace and war.

I spent many years and my children grew up to be mighty men, each one having his tribe in subjection. The envoy who went north or south to the Residence tarried with me [*i.e.*, the messenger of the Pharaoh passing through Syria on his official journeys]. I gave water to the thirsty, set upon the road him that had strayed, and rescued him that had been plundered. When the Bedouins began to wax bold and to withstand the chieftains of the lands, I counselled (?) their movements. The Prince of Retenu caused me to pass many years as captain of his host, and every country against which I marched, when I made my attack, it was driven from its pastures and its wells. . . .

There came a mighty man of Retenu, that he might challenge me in my camp. He was a champion without peer, and had subdued the whole of Retenu. He vowed that he would fight me, and planned to rob me; he plotted to take my cattle as a spoil, by the counsel of his tribe. That prince communed with me and I said: "I know him not; forsooth, I am no confederate of his, that I should stride about his encampment. Or have I ever opened his door or overthrown his fence? Nay, it is envy, because he seeth me doing thy behest. Assuredly I am like a bull of the cattle in the midst of a strange herd, and the steer of the kine attacketh him, and the long-horned bull chargeth (?)."

*I am even so a foreigner whom none loveth, any more than a Bedouin would be loved in the Delta. But if that man is a bull and loveth combat, I also am a fighting bull and am not afraid to try conclusions with him.* If his heart be set on fighting, let him speak his will. Doth God not know what is ordained for him? . . .

At night-time I strung my bow and shot my arrows. I drew out my dagger and burnished my weapons. At dawn when Retenu came, it had stirred up its tribes, it had assembled the countries of a half of it, and it had planned this combat. Every heart burned for me; the men's wives jabbered, and every heart was sore for me. They said, "Is there another mighty man who can fight against him?"

Then his shield, his axe, and his armful of javelins. . . . But after I had drawn out his weapons, I caused his arrows to pass by me, uselessly sped. As one approached the other, he charged me, and I shot him, my arrow sticking in his neck. He cried out and fell on his nose. I laid him low with his own axe, and raised my shout of victory on his back. Every Asiatic bellowed. I offered praise to Month, and his following mourned for him. The prince Nenshi, the son of Amu, took me in his embrace.

The years pass, and Sinuhe is seized with longing for his own land. At this point the writer breaks into poetry:

Once a fugitive fled in his season—
   now the report of me is in the Residence.
Once a laggard lagged because of hunger—
   now I give bread to my neighbour.
Once a man left his country because of nakedness—
   now I am shining white in raiment and linen.

Once a man sped for lack of one to send—
  now I have slaves in plenty.
Fair is my house, wide my dwelling-place,
  and I am remembered in the palace.

Then follows a moving prayer, addressed not to any
particular god in the Egyptian pantheon, not to Amun, or
Ptah, or Horus, but simply to "God":

> O God, whosoever thou art, that didst ordain this
> flight, be merciful and bring me again to the Resi-
> dence. Peradventure thou wilt suffer me to see the
> place wherein my heart dwelleth. What is a greater
> matter than that my corpse should be buried in the
> land where I was born? Come to mine aid! May good
> befall, may God show me mercy. . . .
>     O may the king of Egypt show me mercy, that I
> may live by his mercy. May I ask the Lady of the
> Land [5] that is in his palace what her will is. May I hear
> the behests of her children. . . .

The King sends a kindly message to Sinuhe, asking
him to return to Egypt, for he has nothing to fear:

> What hast thou done that aught should be done
> against thee? Thou didst not curse, that thy speech
> should be reproved, and thou didst not so speak in the
> council of the magistrates that thy utterances should
> be thwarted. . . .

[5] The Queen.

And he mentions the Queen, who seems to have had a special regard for the exile:

> But this thine heaven,[6] that is in the palace, yet abideth and prospereth to-day; *she hath her part* in the kingdom of the land, and her children are in the council-chamber. Thou wilt long subsist on the good things they will give thee. . . .

Sinuhe gratefully acknowledges the King's message and after so many years abroad, returns to Egypt, and presents himself before Pharaoh. At first he is seized with trembling, and prostrates himself before Sesostris, unable to speak:

> Then said His Majesty to one of these Chamberlains, "Raise him up. Let him speak to me." And His Majesty said, "See, thou art returned, after thou hast trodden the foreign lands. . . . Eld assaileth thee and thou hast reached old age. It is no small matter that thy body be laid in the ground, and that the barbarians bury thee not. But be not silent, be not silent; speak, thy name is pronounced."

Eventually Sinuhe, who is still dressed in his Asiatic clothes, manages to stammer out a few words of thanks and apology:

> "Behold I am in thy presence. Thine is life and Thy Majesty will do as it pleaseth thee."

[6] The Queen.

Then the royal children were caused to be ushered in. Said His Majesty to the Queen: "See, this is Sinuhe, who hath come back as an Asiatic, a creature of the Bedouins." She uttered an exceeding loud cry, and the royal children shrieked out together. They said unto His Majesty, "Is it really he?" And His Majesty said, "It is really he. . . ."

In a passage which reminds one of the scene in Book VI of the *Odyssey* in which the travel-worn Odysseus bathes and renews himself before going to meet King Alcinous, the story ends with Sinuhe's transformation into an Egyptian again:

And I was placed in the house of a king's son, in which there was noble equipment, and a bath was therein and . . . Precious things of the Treasury were in it, garments of royal linen, myrrh, and fine oil of the king. Counsellors whom he loveth were in every chamber, and every serving man was at his task. Years were made to pass away from my body, I was shaved, and my hair was combed. A load of dirt was given over to the desert, and the [filthy] clothes of the Sand-farers. And I was arrayed in finest linen and annointed with the best oil. I slept on a bed, and gave up the sand to them that be in it, and the oil of wood to him that smeareth himself therewith. . . .

He is given a sumptuous house, but more important to an Egyptian, his "Eternal Habitation"—his tomb—is prepared:

And there was constructed for me a pyramid out of stone within the precinct of the pyramids. The chief architect began the building of it, the painter designed in it, the master-sculptor carved in it, the master-builders of the necropolis busied themselves with it. All the glistening gear that is placed in a tomb-shaft, its needs were supplied therefrom. . . . It was His Majesty who caused it to be made. There is no humble man for whom the like has been done.

And so live I, rewarded by the King, until the day of my death cometh.

I am sorry that for reasons of space I have had partly to summarize this delightful tale, and also that I have not room for further examples of Egyptian prose literature. I have quoted these few examples only to show the kind of stories and poems which educated Egyptians liked to read or hear spoken, in the hope that readers will be led to the rich sources from which they are drawn—books such as Erman's *Literature of the Ancient Egyptians* and other works listed in the Bibliography.

To my mind, the imaginative literature of Ancient Egypt can bring us nearer to the Pharaoh's people even than their works of art. But a word of warning: though much of their literature is rewarding, a great deal is tedious, clumsy, and obscure. I recommend the folk tales; the biographical romances, such as "The Voyage of Wenamun"; the love poems (which have a lovely lyric sweetness); and the best of the religious verse, especially Akhnaten's "Hymn to the Aten."

But the Egyptians were not a mystical people, and

even in their highest flights they never approached the
intensity and beauty of Hebrew poetry. If you doubt this,
read the finest Egyptian poem you can find on their
favorite subject—mortality—and compare it with

. . . When they shall be afraid of that which is
high, and fears shall be in the way, and the almond
tree shall flourish, and the grasshopper shall be a
burden, and desire shall fail; because man goeth to his
long home, and the mourners go about the streets.

Or ever the silver cord be loosed, or the golden
bowl be broken, or the pitcher be broken at the foun-
tain, or the wheel broken at the cistern.

Then shall the dust return to the earth as it
was; and the spirit shall return unto God who gave
it. . . .

# CHAPTER 10

# LABORERS AND CRAFTSMEN

*I was an artist skilled in my art, pre-eminent in my
learning. . . . I knew (how to represent) the movements of the image of a man and the carriage of a
woman . . . the poising of the arm to bring the
hippotomaus low and the movements of the run-
ner. . . .*
From the tomb of a sculptor (Twelfth Dynasty).

S O far we have dealt mainly with the educated class
which governed Egypt: the great officials, the chiefs
of the Army, the lawyers and taxgatherers, the
priests and the scribes. These, the articulate few, have left
their written records in self-laudatory tomb inscriptions.
But the inarticulate many, the creators of Egypt's wealth—
the builders, the artists and craftsmen, the laborers in field
and workshop—remain dumb save for the few words they
are permitted to say in the tomb paintings of their masters.
Even the master engineers, the men who designed and
planned the pyramids and temples, and those who organized and drilled the great labor force which quarried
the huge blocks of granite for the colossal statues, the
builders of the boats which could carry 650 tons from
Assuan to Memphis, have left us hardly any written records of their methods. Hence the question which springs

to the lips of the wondering visitor when he catches his first glimpse of the Great Pyramid, or the Hypostyle Hall at Karnak, or some tiny gem of craftsmanship in precious metal: *"How* did they do it?"

Fortunately, from the time of the Old Kingdom onwards, a nobleman loved to have depicted on the walls of his tomb the activities of his many servants. From a careful study of these pictures, together with such tools as have survived, Egyptologists have learned a great deal about Egyptian laborers and craftsmen, and the question "How did they do it?" can, in the majority of cases, be satisfactorily answered.

One such nobleman was the Vizier Rekhmire, who, among other things, was responsible for the great estates attached to the Temple of Amun. He was also, as his tomb inscriptions show, in supreme control of the great workshops of the Temple, where one of his sons, Mer-y, was Superintendent. Another son, his eldest, whose name was Menkheperre-Sonb, was Scribe of the Temple Dues. Using only these tomb paintings as our guide, let us follow the Vizier on a tour of inspection.

It is now some weeks since the army of Tuthmosis marched out of Thebes on its way to the land of Retenu. Many young men have followed His Majesty, including Rekhmire's son, Kenamun, and his friend Senmut. With the Pharaoh away, the Vizier finds that his responsibilities, always onerous, are now even heavier, since he is virtually the ruler of the country in the King's absence. Yesterday he received in audience the embassies from Punt, from Keftiu (Crete), from Syria, and from Nubia, bearing tribute which the Vizier received on behalf of his royal master. For hours he had sat on a gilded seat, attended by his retinue, while the foreigners filed past him bearing their tribute on their shoulders, and the scribes had noted down the names and numbers of the objects for the records. First the Cretans—slim, dark men with black, curling hair and a proud bearing—carrying the products of the Cretan workshops:

> One vase of lapis-lazuli fitted with golden bands and handles . . . ten blocks of silver . . . one gold dish . . . a lioness's head in gold . . . the head of a crested bird in gold . . . a drinking cup of gold with an ibex's head . . . a lion's head in gold . . . a large two-handled silver vase . . . a dagger in a blue sheath. . . .

The voice of the scribe droned on monotonously, and Rekhmire, nodding on his throne, might well have asked, "Will the line stretch out to the crack of doom?"

Then came the dark-skinned Nubians from the south, with their characteristic offerings: ostrich feathers and eggs, logs of ebony, gold bars, leopard skins, ivory tusks, and the skins of giraffes. Afterwards came the led animals: leopards, baboons, and giraffes for the Royal Zoo. Then came slaves, mainly women and children, to work as weavers in the Temple workshops.

On the day previous to the receiving of foreign tribute Rekhmire had presided in the Hall of Judgment, for one of his many offices corresponded to that of Lord Chief Justice. That had been even more exhausting, for there had been many litigants and the day had been hot. When he was a younger man, Rekhmire had been proud to receive this appointment and had resolved to live up to the highest ideals of justice. Indeed, he had had these ideals boldly set down on the walls of his tomb: ". . . dispensing justice impartially and seeing to it that the two litigants are contented, judging between poor and well to do alike, no petitioner weeping because of him. . . ."

But as he had sat, hour after hour, in the crowded hall, listening to the disputes of the advocates, hearing, in the corridors outside, the voices of other litigants clamoring for admission, he had been conscious of a great weariness of spirit. Some of his minor officials took bribes, he knew, and he had tried to stop the practice. But it still went on. Also it was all very well to "judge between the poor and well to do alike," but what if the well to do had influence at Court? And Rekhmire had many enemies. Still, he had done his best, and, as a guide to his successors in office, had set out at some length on the walls of his tomb "the duties of a Vizier." One fragment read:

It is he who hears the case regarding any deficit in the Temple dues. It is he who assesses any assessment in kind for anyone who has to pay one to him. It is he who hears all law cases. It is he who allows reductions in the imposts on places or industry. . . . It is he who opens the House of Gold in connection with the High Treasurer. It is he who inspects the tribute of Byblos. . . . It is he who inspects the water-supply on the first of every ten-day period. . . . He it is who fits out ships according as anyone is fitted for it. He

it is who despatches any messenger of the Royal
Demesne . . . when the monarch is on an expedition. . . .

"And the monarch *always* seems to be on an expedition," sighs Rekhmire, reflecting on the number of times
he has watched the King march out of Thebes. And he
smiles as he remembers a phrase which he has had inserted
in the tomb inscription, a true phrase, but one which had
surprised some people:

Lo, as to [the position of a] vizier, lo, it is not
pleasant at all; *no, it is bitter as gall.* . . .

But today is the day of his routine visit to the workshops of Amun, of which Rekhmire's son, Mer-y, is superintendent. The Vizier, who has always worked with his
brain, has a great admiration for manual craftsmanship and
enjoys watching the making of beautiful things. He also
has definite ideas on working methods and has described
himself in his tomb as *"giving instruction to each man regarding his duties in the routine of all manner of produc-
tion."* Mer-y does not always agree with him, but then,
sons always think they know better than their fathers. The
chariots bearing the Vizier and his retinue sweep through
the ceremonial gateway, and draw up outside the Temple
workshops. Preceded and followed by fanbearers, Rekhmire
enters.

The workshops are large and noisy. There is a continual
din of hammers, saws and drills, and a great variety of
smells—of wood shavings, oil, burning metal, and sweat.

166

Mer-y, a tall, serious-faced young man in a black wig and carrying a wand of office, accompanies his father from room to room. They go first to the jewelers' shop. Here are men shaping and polishing beads of malachite, carnelian, lapis lazuli, and other semiprecious stones. They use a fine bronze drill for making the holes, revolved by looping a bowstring around the shaft of the drill and then drawing the bow rapidly to and fro. At another bench a craftsman is setting tiny fragments of glass to make an elaborate inlay in a gold pectoral. The stones being used, and lying near the workman's hands, come from many parts of Asia: crystal and chalcedony from the Eastern Desert, turquoise from Sinai, lapis lazuli from western Asia. But you will look in vain for precious stones: no diamonds, rubies, sapphires, or opals.

Rekhmire picks up the gold pectoral and scrutinizes the inlay.

"Glass," he says scornfully, putting it down. "In our ancestors' time, my son, they'd have used turquoise and amethyst! *What* an age!" And he walks on.

In the next room workmen are boring out stone vases with a heavy stone drill, worked by a crank at the top and weighted to help the drill to bite. Drills are sometimes of stone, sometimes of copper, but the Egyptians did *not* have a method of making copper any harder than we can make it today, in spite of the oft-repeated legend. So there was an enormous wastage of metal when drilling or cutting hard stones.

They pass on to the carpenters' shop. A number of articles have been laid out for the Vizier's inspection: a fan handle, an inlaid casket for funerary equipment, a statue of ebony with gilt mountings, and a silvered mace-head. Rekhmire fingers the objects, then moves closer to watch the men at work. At one end of the room two men are sawing logs into planks. The log is lashed to a stake and one man inserts wedges in the cut to keep it open. The saw cuts on the *pulling*, not the pushing stroke (see illustration on Plate 36).

Nearby another carpenter is sawing the planks into appropriate lengths for the cabinetmaker. Look at the cabinetmaker's tools. He has a simple chisel, a deep, narrow mortise chisel, an axe, an adze (which he uses instead of a plane), a clublike hammer, a mallet, an awl (used, in conjunction with a bow, for boring), a straightedge, a bench with a rectangular slot, a flanged square for checking the angles, and a miter block. Any modern carpenter who found himself back in Ancient Egypt in 1500 B.C. would be quite at home with most of these tools, except perhaps, the hammer, which had no handle.

Here a man is heating glue over a fire while stucco is being ground with a piece of red sandstone. There two men are applying the stucco to a box; afterwards it will be gilded. Rekhmire is particularly interested in a shrine of cedarwood, decorated in ebony, which is being made by four men. One man is carving the recesses into which the ebony inlays are to be placed while his companion carefully shapes the inlays, smoothing them with semicircular pieces of white sandstone, which perform the same function as modern sandpaper. Rekhmire has had a hand in this design, or likes to think so. His hand caresses the polished wood. "A lovely piece of cedar," he says, suddenly remembering the slopes of the Lebanon above Byblos with a pain at the heart. "I wonder," he thinks "if I shall ever see it again. . . ."

At the same time he makes a mental note to add a phrase to the scene of the Temple workshops he is having prepared in his tomb.

*"This noble, who guides the hands of his work-men . . ."* Would that do? No; better make it:

> *"This noble, who lays down principles and guides the hands of his workmen, making furniture of ivory and ebony, ssndm wood, mrw wood, and true cedar from the mountain slopes of Lebanon. . . ."*

He is still running his fingers absent-mindedly along the surface of the ebony inlay when his son calls to him from the far end of the room.

"Father! Don't you want to see the metalworkers?"

"Of course."

In actual fact, he doesn't, because the day is very hot and he hates furnaces and molten metal. But today they are casting the great bronze pivots for the new gates of the Temple, so he enters the smoke-blackened room of the smiths, followed by members of his suite, who walk delicately for fear of spoiling their spotless white linen.

There is so much noise that Mer-y has to raise his voice when explaining the process to his father. Apart from the clanging of hammers, there is a loud, intermittent roaring from several charcoal fires, beside each of which stands an almost naked man, operating a pair of foot bellows. He leans first on one foot and then on the other, pulling up the deflated bellows with a rope. With each blast from the nozzle, which is fixed in the heart of the fire, the flame leaps and the sparks fly up. The courtiers mop their brows and look unhappy.

On the ground is a large mold of burned clay, made in the shape of a heavy top door pivot and its fitting, together with the angle piece and pivot for the bottom. Nearby stand jars containing copper and tin mixed in the correct proportions. There are seventeen pouring vents in the mold, and the operation is one of some delicacy, because if one man is not ready he can wreck the whole work. But all goes well. The copper and tin are placed in clay crucibles, one over each hearth, and when the metals have melted, men come forward and with ordered, disciplined movements at the foreman's words of command, pour out the liquid bronze into the seventeen vents. Each section of the huge bronze gates will be made in this way, then fitted together, polished, and finally plated with pure gold. In this operation Rekhmire finds another scene for his tomb frescoes (see illustration on Plate 35).

In another part of the workshops metal beaters are working with gold and silver. At the far end of the chamber the raw material, in the form of gold rings, is being accurately weighed before being issued to the smiths. Afterwards each manufactured article will be weighed to see that its weight tallies with that of the original issue of metal. The Vizier nods his approval at this careful precaution against theft.

The first operation is to beat the metal into flat plates, using a "maul" of hard stone. Then from the flat plate the vases are hammered into shape over a stout rod of metal fixed in the ground, the rod being provided with changeable heads—flat, curved, or angular, to suit the work. Where necessary, joints are then soldered, the operator holding the part in a pair of tongs and using a blowpipe to obtain the required high temperature. (For these and other illustrations of the workshops, see Plates 35, 36, and 37.)

Rekhmire and his followers are glad to leave the overheated smithies, but the Vizier's duties are not yet completed. Bidding farewell to his son, he drives to the quayside to watch the unloading of huge blocks of limestone which have been shipped upriver from Memphis. The great Temple of Amun-Re at Karnak is always being altered and enlarged. Every King of Egypt tries to outdo his predecessors in honoring the King of Gods, and Tuthmosis III is no exception. One ship, about 150 feet long, is already moored alongside the quay. Another approaches, the crew slackening the sail, paying out ropes and dropping anchor stones. In the other ships men are poling their craft along to the anchorage, while a lookout man in the bows marks the depth of the water with a sounding pole.

The Vizier stays to watch the unshipping of one load and then, after a word with the chief of the stevedores, climbs into his chariot and is driven home.

That little sketch, based solely on the evidence of Rekhmire's tomb paintings, explains the working techniques of certain types of Egyptian craftsmen at one period of Dynastic history. Whole books could be—and have been—written on Egyptian arts and crafts. For those who wish to study this subject in more detail there are some useful studies by Petrie, such as his *Arts and Crafts in Ancient Egypt* and his *Tools and Weapons*, though both these are now out of date, and should be read with caution. However, Petrie is reliability itself compared with

> . . . the statements and theories printed by engineers, architects, and other technicians, after a brief visit to the monuments of Egypt, which would never have appeared had they consulted the archaeologist.

So writes Mr. R. Engelbach, late of the Antiquities Department of the Egyptian Government, in his chapter on "Mechanical and Technical Processes and Materials" in *The Legacy of Egypt,* which I have found the most useful and reliable short guide to this subject. Not being a professional archaeologist myself, I know how easy it is to be led away on false, though attractive, trails. Ancient Egypt, unfortunately, is still the happy hunting ground of a certain type of crank, and unless one is careful to stick to the best authorities, one may find oneself wallowing in "lost arts," "occult practices," theories of reincarnation, and all the hocus-pocus which prevents one from getting at the truth, which to me is far more wonderful than any fantasy.

Let us take a few examples, starting with stone quarrying. Anyone who has admired the great obelisk in the Place de la Concorde in Paris, or the granite colossi in our great museums, will have wondered how the Ancient Egyptians quarried these huge blocks of stone without the aid of blasting powder, or even of hard cutting tools (for iron tools were not used until comparatively late in Egyptian history). Incredible though it may seem, these huge blocks, often of granite or other hard rock, were *jarred* from their native rock by pounding it with balls of dolerite, used as hammers. Sometimes copper chisels were used with a mallet.

The method for cutting large blocks of granite was to

. . . detach the parent mass first by pounding with balls or hammers, made of some hard, resilient stone such as dolerite, held in the hand, and then by the use of wedges. In this connection, it must be remembered that the pounding ball does not pound or bruise away the stone any more than does the blunt-pointed pick of the modern mason. It jars off pieces of stone by vibration, and the efficiency of the work depends on the quality of the blow; one strength alone does the job; harder or lighter blows have no effect [Engelbach].

Once detached from the parent mass of rock, the colossal statue was pounded into rough shape by the same method, then levered on to a heavy wooden sled and dragged by hundreds of men to the workshops. (In a tomb fresco at El-Barsha 172 men were shown dragging such a colossus.) If the workshops were some distance away, the block would be dragged onto a ship, or perhaps a raft, and floated downriver. In the shops men worked on it with tools of ever-decreasing size. Then tubular drills were brought into use, *e.g.*, for the eyes, or the rounded corners of hieroglyphs; if small, they were rotated by means of a bowstring (as explained above) or if large, by hand and loaded with weights. "Although no tubular drills have been found," says Engelbach, "the eyes of several statues show traces of them, of graduated sizes, and the bottoms of the holes prove that the metal must have been of extraordinary thinness. The nature of the abrasive is a matter for speculation. . . ."

For the final shaping of the statue, metal tools were used, but as these were of copper, which could only be annealed to the hardness of mild steel, the expenditure of metal must have been very great. But nothing is known about the material and methods the Egyptians used for giving the statues their wonderful polish.

They also used bronze saws, which could cut hard rock, such as granite and basalt. I have seen cuts over a yard long which imply the use of a saw at least 6 feet in length. Again some kind of abrasive must have been used, but we have no means of knowing what it was.

These methods were used as far back as the Old Kingdom (2780–2100 B.C.) and even earlier.

The Egyptians used several types of stone: limestone, which extends from Cairo to beyond Esna; a very fine-grained limestone, hard and marblelike, from Qâw and Beni Hassan; sandstone; and granite of several varieties, pink, grey and black. Alabaster was also quarried, chiefly from Hatnub, near Tell-el-Amarna. The main quarry for basalt, which was often used for paving the temples of the Old Kingdom, was apparently at Faiyum.

The chief source of supply for granite was Assuan in Upper Egypt, where one can see how the Ancient Egyptians split their huge building blocks from the parent rock by means of wedges. The method was to cut a gallery into which a man could climb. Then, with a hard, blunt-pointed tool like a mason's pick he would work downwards, cutting narrow, vertical trenches, one at the back, and one on each side, leaving the block detached on all sides except the base. The next step was to make deep wedge slots at the base of the block, and then drive in metal wedges with a hammer until the block split away from its base and could be removed. Sometimes, when the wedge slots were in a position in which it was impossible to deliver a heavy blow, another method was used to split the rock. Wooden wedges were driven in tightly, then soaked in water. After a while the wood expanded and split the rock. Engelbach experimented with this method and found the wood expanded in ten hours.

At Assuan one can see thousands of these wedge slots, some of great size. Egyptians of a later generation than the pyramid-builders, when demolishing their ancestors' monuments, used the same method for splitting the granite blocks into more convenient sizes. (See the illustration on Plate oo, taken near one of the pyramids at Abusir.)

But long before the blocks were hewn from the quarry and shaped by the masons, other men must have worked out quite complicated arithmetical and geometrical calculations to establish the volume of building material which would be needed—for, say, a pyramid of given size—and the building itself would have been laid out with the utmost precision. For instance, they measured the angle of slope by the horizontal offset per unit of vertical height, known as the *seked*. To cut the casing stones to the required angle they would mark off 1 cubit vertically and then set out the *seked* horizontally. Then the mason drew the line which indicated the direction in which the stone should be cut. One of the most fascinating aspects of Egyptian buildings is that, in many cases, these mason's lines can still be seen. Also I have seen stone blocks in the quarries still roughly painted with signs indicating names of the quarrying gangs which were responsible for them.

Such relics bring us very near to the workmen of Ancient Egypt. I remember, during my last visit to Egypt, going to Sakkara to see part of the newly discovered pyramid which Mr. Zakaria Goneim had unearthed at Sakkara, a building dating from about 2700 B.C. It was probably built by Sekhem-khet, a successor of King Djoser, who built the Step Pyramid, the oldest stone building in the world. Goneim had excavated a considerable length of a boundary wall, which had evidently been abandoned and buried after being built to a height of about 15 feet. Sand had covered it for five thousand years, preserving the fine limestone surface. And on that white limestone wall, the blocks of which looked as if they had been cut yesterday, was a thin red line near the base, indicating the horizontal. The masons had dipped a length of cord in red paint, stretched it, and slapped it against the wall, just as a modern mason does today.

Even more extraordinary were the crude drawings— also in red paint, which some of the workmen had daubed on the wall in an idle moment; a lion hunt with "pin-men" pursuing the animal with spears, and a portrait of a Libyan with his long and, to the workmen, outlandish robe and tall headdress. This was such a man as they must have seen sometimes hovering on the desert fringes. Standing in the newly excavated trench and looking at these drawings on the sunlit, white wall, I felt as if the workmen of Sekhem-khet had just gone off for their lunch and would be back at any moment.

Although no mathematical documents have survived which apply to the construction of a particular building, such documents as the Rhind Mathematical show the kind of problems which were tackled and solved. Mr. R. W. Sloley, in *The Legacy of Egypt*, cites a few examples, expressed in modern terminology:

> *Problem:* A triangle of given area has the perpendicular height 2½ times the base. Find the base and height. . . .
>
> *Comment:* It seems certain that the properties of the isosceles, if not of any triangle, now expressed by the formulae which follow, were known; but it is not easy to prove this conclusion from the material available:

$$A = \frac{bh}{2} \; : \quad b = \sqrt{2\left(\frac{Ah}{b}\right)} \; : \quad b = \frac{b}{h}\sqrt{\left(2A\frac{h}{b}\right)}$$

where $A$ = area, $b$ = base and $h$ = height.

Another example quoted by Sloley:

> *Problem:* Find the area of a circular field 9 cubits in diameter.
>
> *Comment:* The working (out of the problem in the papyrus) implies the use of the following rule: Subtract ⅑ from the diameter and square the result. This is equivalent to a value of $\pi$ (ratio of circumference to diameter) of 3.1605. The fact that the area is expressed as a square points to the method of counting squares on a surface ruled in squares, in order to arrive at the approximation to $\pi$ known as 3.1415.

I apologize to nonmathematical readers who, like myself, find this somewhat puzzling. It should, at any rate, increase their respect for the Ancient Egyptians, as it did mine.

A knowledge of mathematics was also necessary to solve problems connected with the supply of material, the allotment of labor, and the feeding of troops or workmen. Let us go back for a moment to our friend Hori, the scribe mentioned in Chapter VII. It was he who had to reprimand his subordinate Amenemope, the "Scribe of the Army," for his lack of knowledge of military matters. In another part of the same papyrus he challenges Amenemope to tell him how to calculate the amount of material needed to build a ramp:

> For see, thou art the clever scribe who is at the head of troops! A ramp is to be constructed, 730 cubits long, 55 cubits wide, containing 120 compartments, and filled with reeds and beams; 60 cubits high at its summit, 30 cubits in its middle, with a . . . of 15 cubits, and its . . . 5 cubits. The quantity of bricks needed for it is asked of the generals, and the scribes are all collected together, without one of them knowing anything. They all put their trust in thee and say: "Thou art a clever scribe, my friend! Decide for us quickly! Behold thy name is famous; let one be found in this place to magnify the other thirty! Do not let it be said that there is aught thou dost not know. Answer us, how many bricks are needed for it." See, its measurements are before thee. Each one of its compartments is 30 cubits and is 7 cubits broad. . . .

Poor Amenemope! When he has to calculate the amount of food needed by his troops he is even more at sea.

The auxiliary troops which thou commandest number 1,900, (also) 520 Shardana, 1,600 Kehek, 100 Mashawasha, 880 Negroes—in all 5,000, not reckoning their officers. A present hath been brought thee of bread, cattle and wine. The number of men is too great for thee, and the provision is too small for them; 300 wheaten loaves, 1,800 . . . loaves, 120 goats of different kinds, 30 measures of wine—the soldiers are so many and the provision is under-estimated. Thou receivest the provision, and it is placed in the camp. The army is ready and equipped; so divide it up quickly and give to each man his portion. The Bedouins look on furtively and say, *"Sopher yode"* [foreign argot; probably ironical, meaning "O sapient scribe"].

Midday is come; the camp is hot. They say, "It is time to start. Be not wroth, O commandant of the auxiliaries. We have yet far to march," they say. "Why is there no bread? Our night-quarters are far off."

Amenemope, in despair, resorts to beating the men, but they will have their revenge. They will report him to the Ruler.

Approach thou to give the food! *An hour cometh, in which one is* without a scribe from the Ruler. *That thou shouldst take it upon thee* to beat us, that is not good, comrade; he will hear of it and he will send to undo thee. . . .

Any officer who has had charge of the commissariat will sympathize with Amenemope. Perhaps it was not due entirely to his bad arithmetic. More likely another regiment had "liberated" the missing rations.

After that slight digression, let us consider the actual construction of a pyramid. Some of the stone blocks weighed as much as ten tons. Yet so fine was the masonry that, as Petrie wrote,

> . . . the mean thickness of the eastern joint of the northern casing stones [of the Great Pyramid] is 0.020 inch [1⁄50 inch]; therefore the mean variation of the cutting of the stone from a straight line is but 0.01 inch [1⁄100 inch] of 75 inches up the face . . . these joints, with an area of 35 square feet each, were not only worked as finely as this, but cemented throughout. . . .

How were these great blocks maneuvered into position and placed there with such precision? Briefly, the only mechanical aids the Ancient Egyptian workmen had were the lever and the roller. *They did not have the pulley,* so that the blocks could not be hauled up and gently lowered into place. That no pulleys have been found does not, in itself, prove that they did not exist. But other facts lead to this conclusion. For instance, in the many representations of ancient Egyptian ships there are no pulleys at the masthead. The yards had to be *pushed* up; and in some tomb paintings sailors are shown doing this. Again, if pulleys had been used, tongs or "lewises" would have been needed to grab the blocks and would have left marks. No such marks have been found.

The method of construction seems to have been as follows: first, the foundations were leveled by "running a watercourse along and about the surface to be leveled, and then measuring down from the surface at many points simultaneously, thus establishing datum points to which the complete surface would be eventually reduced" (Engelbach). This would explain the slight error which exists in the level of the platform which runs partly under the Great Pyramid. It is on a perfect plane, but slopes up about 6 inches from the northeast to the southeast corner. If when the points were being checked, a northeast wind had been blowing, this would have produced the error.

The stones were dragged on wooden sleds up the causeway leading to the pyramid, and the first course laid on the virgin rock. When the top had been leveled the workmen were ready for the next course. They built a ramp leading up to the top of the first course, and up this they dragged the blocks, levering them into position. While that course was being laid, the ramp would be built up and extended, getting longer and longer with each course, since the angle of incline would have to remain the same. Engelbach believes that the reason for the thin layer of mortar between the blocks was not to hold them in position (their weight alone would have been sufficient) but because there was no other way in which a block weighing several tons could have been pushed "home" against its neighbor, "unless it were, so to speak, floating on a thin bed of wet, viscid mortar. I believe that this is the explanation of the mortar and the almost perfect smoothness of the tops."

Similar methods must have been used in building the temples with their pillars and pylons. It was a matter of careful planning, a few simple mechanical aids, and the organization of abundant man power.

The Egyptians were greatly helped in their building operations by river transport. They rarely had to carry heavy loads great distances overland, since the country bordered the river along its entire length. Boats, as we have seen, played a vital part, and vessels of quite large size were built even in the pre-Dynastic period (before 3200 B.C.). Even in the time of Snofru (Third Dynasty) there is a record of a boat of 100 cubits (172 feet), and by the Eighteenth Dynasty they were carrying loads of more than 650 tons. These vessels were of many types: warships, cattle boats, freighters, and private yachts. . . . There are many representations of boatbuilders, whose craft must have been in continual demand.

However, they were handicapped in the early stages by a lack of suitable timber, since broad planks were unobtainable from such native Egyptian trees as the sycamore fig. Therefore the Egyptian boatbuilders developed a special method of construction, utilizing small planks, which Herodotus saw and described:

> . . . They cut a quantity of planks about 2 cubits [41 inches] in length, arranging the planks like bricks, and attaching them by ties to a number of long stakes or poles till the hull is complete. They give the boat no ribs, but caulk the seams with papyrus from inside.

A series of thwarts prevented the boat from collapsing outward, while stout cables attached at each end and passing over fixed stays in the side of the hull maintained rigidity lengthwise. In boats such as these the Egyptians made long journeys and carried great loads. But one should be-ware of being misled by Ancient Egyptian artists who show 500-ton obelisks lashed to the *decks* of large boats, which would obviously be top-heavy. Most probably these big loads were carried on rafts.

Carpentry, at which the Egyptians were adept, may have developed out of boatbuilding. Complete mastery over wood had been achieved by the time of the First Dynasty, as we know from the elaborately carved and inlaid cabinets which have survived. The native woods were sycamore, willow, tamarisk, *persea*, and *sidder* (Arabic, *nabq*). Cedar and cypress were imported before 3000 B.C., and later they used ebony, fir, yew, and beech. Nearly all the joints used by carpenters today were known five thousand years ago. Third Dynasty coffins exist with halved, mitered, and con-cealed miter joints. During the same period (2800 B.C.) the Egyptians were making plywood consisting of six different layers of different woods. Nails were usually wooden pegs, but tiny gold nails were used for affixing veneers. Tenon and mortise joints were also known at this early period, and were much used for the joining of the narrow planks which were all that could be obtained from native timber. The chariots are fine examples of the carpenter's art, light and strong, with double spokes.

Practically the only modern carpenter's tool which the Ancient Egyptian did not possess was the plane, but he could do such fine work with the adze that he did not need it. Many examples of these tools have been preserved in Egyptian tombs—squares, levels, chisels, mallets, and saws —which differ very little from their modern counterparts (see illustration on Plate 39).

And yet by the learned scribes of Ancient Egypt these

brilliant craftsmen were held in low esteem. The *Literature of the Ancient Egyptians* has this translation of a poem of the Middle Kingdom written about the metalworker:

> I have never seen the smith as an ambassador,
>     or the goldsmith carry tidings;
> Yet I have seen the smith at his work
> At the mouth of his furnace,
> His fingers were like crocodile [hide]
> He stank more than the roe of fish. . . .

And of the wood carver the same poet writes:

> Each artist who works with the chisel
> Tires himself more than he who hoes [a field]
> The wood is his field, of metal are his tools.
>     In the night—is he free?
> He works more than his arms are able,
> In the night—he lights a light.[1]

The men and women who wove the clothes which the Egyptians wore are unsung, yet throughout the long span of Egyptian civilization theirs was a highly important craft employing hundreds of thousands. Erman says:

. . . They lavished all their skill in the one endeavour to prepare the finest and whitest linen that was possible, and they certainly brought their linen to great perfection; I need only remind my readers of the

[1] In our own age the scribe is more likely to burn the midnight oil than the artisan.—L.C.

184

white garments worn by men of rank, which were so fine that their limbs could be seen gleaming through them. Some of this very fine linen that we possess is almost comparable to our silken materials for smoothness and softness.

Cotton, of course, was unknown, so that the weaving industry involved only the weaving of linen. They cultivated flax from very early times, boiling it in a large vessel which is represented in Middle Kingdom tomb paintings. The idea was to free the outer covering of the stalks, and afterwards they were beaten with hammers until the outside was loosened or destroyed. The flax which was thus obtained had then to be cleaned and separated from the rubbish before it could be used. In the Middle Kingdom this process was carried out by hand: men are shown carefully picking out the good fibers and laying them together to form a thread. But in the time of Rekhmire the weavers used a comb, as is done today.

There are some interesting examples of weavers' looms and shuttles in the British Museum which show that in principle the method was basically the same as that used today, but, of course, everything was done by hand. The thread was moistened, and then twisted together with a spindle. Close by on the ground stood a pot containing the rough threads; the person spinning allowed the thread to run over his or her hand or over a fork. Great skill was shown. In one picture we see women managing two spindles at the same time, and twisting each of the two threads from two different kinds of flax. They managed to do this by balancing themselves on a stool after first removing practically every stitch of clothing so that the two spindles and the threads should not get entangled in their dresses.

The Egyptians were also highly skilled in the treatment of animal skins. Beautiful skins, especially those which were spotted or patterned, were used in the manufacture of seat coverings, shields, and quivers. Panther skins seem to have been especially valued.

However, only the rich could afford the fine linen garments. The poor would have to be content with the coarsest material or the hides of animals.

Other arts in which the Egyptians excelled were rope-making (necessary for the hauling of huge monuments), faïence and glassmaking. Specimens exist of rope made from palm fiber 5 inches thick. These ropes are as strong and well made as any made today. Faïence reached a very high standard; it was made from finely powdered quartz mixed with an adhesive (probably natron) and then fired. The Egyptians used it for vases and making statuettes, such as the well-known *shawabti* figures which are found in hundreds in the tombs. They also made glass objects, but glass blowing did not come into use until Roman times. The Egyptian method was to wind drawn rods of glass round a cone, then reheat, roll, and polish. Or it could be cast, as in the case of the beautiful glass headrest found in Tutankhamun's tomb. Gold was mined in enormous quantities in Nubia and elsewhere, and the art of the Egyptian goldsmith at its best approaches the finest work of the Italian Renaissance. Gold was used for plating an immense variety of objects, and such a vast quantity was available that Tushratta, King of Mittani, could write to Amenophis IV (Akhnaten):

Send me much gold, more gold, for in my brother's [*i.e.*, Akhnaten's] land gold is as common as dust. . . .

The solid gold coffin of Tutankhamun, one of the greatest masterpieces of Ancient Egyptian art, weighs 300 pounds avoirdupois. In the time of Sheshonq of the Twentieth Dynasty the weight of gold and silver given to the Temple amounted to more than 20 tons.

These lovely things pay perpetual tribute to the skill of the Egyptian craftsmen. We can marvel at the magnificent gold mask of Tutankhamun; we shall never know who made it (see illustration on Plate 41). The thousands who toiled on the pyramids, who raised the drum columns in the Hypostyle Hall at Karnak, who fashioned the alabaster vases, the inlaid ebony and ivory caskets, the necklaces of carnelian and lapis lazuli, have only these things as their memorial. Only occasionally an archaeologist finds in a rubbish-tip near the pyramids a scrap of rope, a workman's basket, or few copper tools, mute witnesses of the anonymous millions who labored for the few.

# CHAPTER 11

## MAGIC AND MEDICINE

S EVERAL months have passed, and again we are in the great house of the Vizier Rekhmire. But the atmosphere is now very different from that which we remember from our last visit. There is no sound of music from the women's quarters; the servants go about their tasks quietly, and no one sings. When we meet Rekhmire walking across the courtyard with his wife, they look grave. For Nofret, the Vizier's eldest daughter, has been stricken down with a fever.

Let us follow the parents as they enter their daughter's bedchamber. Several other members of the family are there: Ta-kha'et with her husband Sinuhe (for since we last met them they have been married) ; and the eldest son, Menkheperre-Sonb, and his wife. They stand a little apart from the bed on which Nofret lies. Her face is flushed and shiny with sweat. She puts her hand to her brow and moans; every now and again her slim body is convulsed with a rigor, and she says, "I am cold. . . . I am cold. . . ."

Near her stands the Court Physician with his assistants. But he is not looking at Nofret. He is leaning over a small table on which stands a magical amulet, a knotted cord, and small jars containing drugs. He makes magical passes over the amulet and the cord, rapidly repeating a spell while one of his assistants makes responses. After a while he takes the amulet and fastens it to the girl's dress, above her heart. Then he ties the cord loosely around her forehead. After more movements of his hands above the body of his patient, he moves across the room to the waiting relatives. Together they leave the room, leaving only a serving-woman to watch over the sick girl.

"Within a day and a night, if Amun is merciful," he says, "the demon will have left her. . . ."

Five hundred miles away, in a desert valley near the Orontees, Senmut, the officer of charioteers, lies unconscious in a tent. A few hours ago, while commanding the rear guard, he had run into an ambush in a narrow defile. The Bedouins had rolled rocks down onto the track, blocking the way, and then poured down on the Pharaoh's Army while they were still in column of route. Unable to maneuver, the charioteers had had to dismount and fight it out hand to hand. It had been a desperate struggle in which young Kenamun had distinguished himself by his courage and intelligence.

Early in the fight the enemy had noted Senmut, whose rank was easily distinguished by his dress and by his standard-bearer, and had marked him out for special attack. Both he and his charioteer were wounded by the first flight of arrows; the horses were killed and the chariot overturned. Half blinded by blood, Senmut had found himself surrounded by Bedouin spearmen. He had killed two before a third brought him down with a mace blow to the side of the helmet. Senmut fell just as Kenamun, who had seen his plight, fought his way through to him with a band of spearmen and drove off the Bedouins. But before doing this he had sent a few bold warriors, including trumpeters, to fight their way out of the ambush and warn the main body of the Army. A few had got through; Tuthmosis heard the trumpets far off along the valley and had sent infantry to the rescue. The Bedouins had been driven off into the hills after heavy slaughter, leaving a hundred dead and dying. Then Kenamun brought his friend's unconscious body to the tent of the Chief Physician. He is standing by now, an anxious look on his own bandaged face as he watches the great man performing an operation by the light of oil lamps.

There is no magic here. First the physician cleans out the arrow wounds, staunches the flow of blood, and neatly stitches the severed flesh. He makes a careful examination and finds that Senmut's left arm and leg are paralyzed. He examines the abrasion on the skull, ascertains that there is no fracture, but recognizes that the paralysis is due to pressure on the brain which must be relieved.

His surgical instruments lie on a table beside the bed: curved knives of various shapes, drills, and saws. With a small sharp saw, he removes a portion of the skull and cuts away the membrane so that the brain lies exposed. Delicately removing the clotted blood and cleaning the damaged tissues, he stitches the membrane back in place, replaces the piece of skull, and binds it in position with bandages and adhesive.

It is already dawn when he rises to his feet; the neighing of horses and the distant braying of trumpets come faintly across the still air. In answer to Kenamun's unspoken question, the doctor says, "I cannot say. It is too early to tell."

He places his hand on Senmut's chest.

"His heart is good. He may survive. But he cannot be moved for a long time. He must stay here for some weeks; then perhaps he can be moved to Kadesh."

Smiling at Kenamun's anxious face, he drops his hand on the young man's shoulder and remarks, "Don't worry, my son. Like all you soldiers, he has a very thick skull. . . ."

Fanciful? Not at all. Such operations were performed by the Ancient Egyptians, even in pre-Dynastic times, and a number of skulls have been found which bear evidence of trepanning. And the patient sometimes survived, as is proved by the fact that the severed section of the skull had knit to the parent bone. Other operations as delicate as this were performed by Egyptian surgeons, as we know from the Edwin Smith Surgical Papyrus, which dates from the beginning of the New Empire (*c.* 1500 B.C.). This, the oldest book of surgery in the world, contains a total of forty-eight cases of injuries, ranging from the cranium to the lower spine, methodically arranged.

Writing of this magnificent manuscript, Dr. P. G. Sobhy Bey, Emeritus Professor of Medicine and History of Medicine, Fouad I University, says:

Each case is preceded by a brief caption expressing a summary diagnosis, followed by another detailed diagnosis, a brief but clearly formulated prognosis and sometimes the therapy. In most cases a later [Egyptian] commentator added one or more explanatory notes [glosses] to the original text in order to interpret

expressions difficult to understand, or to expound obscure passages containing words or expressions which
have become obsolete since the original text of the
manuscript.

This papyrus must therefore have been one of the
standard textbooks used in the Egyptian medical schools.
It may, in fact, be five thousand years old.

There are other medical papyri, such as the Ebers
Papyrus, which deals with boils, cysts, and the like; and
the Kahûn Papyrus, which is concerned with gynecological
cases. There is also the Chester-Beatty Papyrus, part of
which gives prescriptions and remedies for affections of
the anus and rectum, and the Hearst Papyrus, which contains 250 prescriptions. Other papyri are present in the
British Museum and in Turin. Some of these contain almost
identical sections and seem to have been transcribed from
one master work.

What can we learn from them concerning the Egyptians' knowledge of the human body? First, that they had
a better knowledge of anatomy than other ancient peoples,
due almost certainly to the custom of embalmment and
mummification. Warren R. Dawson, in *The Legacy of
Egypt,* writes:

The custom provided for the first time opportu-
nities for observations in comparative anatomy, for
it enabled its practitioners to recognize the analogies
between the viscera of the human body and those of
animals, the latter long familiar from the time-
honoured custom of cutting up animals for food and

for sacrifice. It is a noteworthy fact that the various hieroglyphic signs representing parts of the body, and especially the internal organs, are pictures of the organs of mammals and not of human beings. This shows that the Egyptians' knowledge of mammalian anatomy was older than their knowledge of that of man, and, further, that they recognised the essential identity of the two by devising signs based on the organs of animals and using them unaltered when referring to the corresponding organs in the human body.

In the ancient language there are no less than two hundred anatomical terms, proving that the Ancient Egyptians could recognize and differentiate between a wide variety of human organs which a less enlightened people would have lumped together. But there were many blanks in their knowledge. On the one hand they did recognize the importance of the heart:

The beginning of the science of the physician; to know the movement of the heart; there are vessels attached to it for every movement of the body. . . .

But on the other hand they did not perceive the circulation of the blood. They had one word to denote muscles, arteries, and veins. The word used for blood vessels communicating with the heart is the same as that used for the muscles. They also thought that the heart was the seat of the intelligence and the emotions, and attached little importance to the brain—except that they had observed that damage to the brain affected certain muscles of the body. So important was the heart considered that the embalmers always replaced it in the body before burial, though they removed the other organs for separate embalmment. However, as Warren Dawson says:

> . . . there remained a nucleus of correctly observed truth which suggests that in very early times a serious attempt was being made to understand the structure and functions of the body and its organs, and the effects of injuries on them. It was observed, for instance (as we learn from the Edwin Smith Papyrus) that the brain is enclosed in a membrane and that its hemispheres are patterned with convolutions; that injury to the brain causes a loss of control over various parts of the body, the tension of the facial muscles and other manifestations . . . that certain injuries can be confidently cured, and others, again, are definitely hopeless.

It may be asked why the Egyptians, who used skilled surgery for the treatment of wounds, resorted to magic when faced with internal disorders which had no obvious cause? Why should Nofret's malaria be treated magically and Senmut's concussion rationally? And remember that there was no clear distinction between magician and physician. They were one and the same. If Senmut had developed malaria, the physician would have applied the same treatment to him as his colleague in Thebes applied to Nofret.

The answer seems to be that where there was no obvious cause for an illness, it was attributed to the presence of evil spirits within the body of the patient. The physician's task then was to drive the demon out, either by conjuration, exorcism, or the application of drugs which were originally chosen for their magical rather than their therapeutic properties. Medicine, in fact, developed out of magic, and it would take a bold man, indeed, to affirm that magic has entirely disappeared from medical practice, even today. Only nowadays we call it "having faith in the doctor."

Thus in Egyptian papyri, such as the Ebers and the Hearst, the doctor harangues the demon within the patient's body, or implies that the suffering is due to some poison emanating from the demon which has lodged in the body of the sufferer. If spells were found ineffective, the next recourse was to concoctions of so repellent a nature as to force the offending spirit to quit. People who complain of having to take unpleasant-tasting medicine may be thankful that they did not live in Ancient Egypt where they might have been expected to swallow crushed (or live) insects, excreta, or various revolting forms of animal or vegetable life. Incidentally, these Ancient Egyptian prescriptions, passing to Europe via Greek, Roman, or Arab medical textbooks, reappeared in the magical formulae of witches in medieval and later periods. Indeed, they survive even today as folk superstitions. The incantation of Macbeth's Weird Sisters might almost have come from an Egyptian doctor's book of prescriptions:

> . . . Eye of newt and toe of frog,
> Wool of bat and tongue of dog
> Adder's fork and blind-worm's sting,
> Lizard's leg and howlet's wing . . .

Scale of dragon, tooth of wolf,
Witches' mummy. . . .

Sir Alan Gardiner, writing of the Egyptian magician's art, has defined two parts of his performance, the *oral rite* and the *manual rite*. In certain of the medical papyri ("medico-magical" would be a better word) there are often directions for the performance of the manual rite (*i.e.,* a ritual) to accompany the preceding oral rite.

The manual rite often took the form of reciting the words over an image of clay, a string of beads, a knotted cord, a piece of inscribed linen . . . or some other object. These objects, thus magically charged, were generally placed upon or attached to the patient's body.

Alternative prescriptions were given if the first failed.

What kind of diseases did the Ancient Egyptians suffer from? We can learn quite a lot from statuary, paintings, and from the examination of mummies. Doctors have identified cases of infantile paralysis, Pott's disease, and rickets. Eye diseases—trachoma and ophthalmia—were common, as they are in modern Egypt. Bilharziasis, the terrible debilitating disease from which more than 80 per cent of the peasant population suffers today—and which is carried by certain species of snails breeding in the irrigation canals—was known in ancient times, and the bilharzia worm has been found in mummies.

The Ancient Egyptians had dental troubles, and were treated by skilled dental surgeons. As Dr. Sobhey Bey, to

196

whom I am indebted for some of the material in this chapter, writes:

> In a tomb of the pyramid period a skull was found showing clear evidence of a successful operation for the drainage of an abscess at the root of the first molar. Another skull showed two teeth skilfully tied together with gold wire, evidently to fasten a loose tooth to its more stable neighbour and so to prevent it falling out. . . .

There were also eye doctors, bowel specialists—"Guardians of the Anus"—and physicians who specialized in internal diseases "who know the secret and specialize in the body fluids." The medical papyri contain prescriptions for treating diseases of the lungs, liver, stomach, bladder, and for various affections of the head and scalp (including recipes for preventing the hair falling out or turning grey). There are prescriptions for rheumatic and arthritic complaints and for women's diseases.

Many of these remedies and prescriptions have been passed on to us via the writings of Pliny, Dioscorides, Galen, and other Greek writers. Dawson writes:

> The works of the classical writers are . . . often merely the stepping-stones by which much of the ancient medical lore reached Europe, apart from direct borrowings. . . . From Egypt we have the earliest medical books, the first observations in anatomy, the first experiments in surgery and pharmacy, the first use of splints, bandages, compresses, and other

appliances, and the first anatomical and medical vo-
cabulary. . . .

So beware of despising the Ancient Egyptians because
their doctors began by using magic. Many of the drugs
they prescribed had genuine therapeutic value, and indeed
are still used in modern pharmacy. For example, acacia,
anise, barley, cassia, castor beans, castor oil, wormwood,
coriander, cucumber, cumin, poppy, and saffron are among
the vegetable substances. Alum, copper, feldspar, sulphur,
red ochre, sodium carbonate and bicarbonate, arsenic and
nitre (the name is Egyptian) have been identified among
the minerals in the medical papyri. And among the animal
substances used were the fats, blood, bone marrow, bile,
liver, and spleen.

Clearly, over thousands of years, those substances
which had proved most successful in the treatment of
particular diseases would always be prescribed for those
diseases; thus scientific medicine grew by degrees out of
magic. Dr. Sobhy Bey disagrees strongly with those who
dismiss most of Egyptian pharmacy as magical hit-or-miss
therapy and little more. Dr. Sobhy, who has the advantage
of being both a distinguished physician and a student of
Egyptology, writes:

. . . The various prescriptions (in the Ebers and
Hearst Papyri) seem to be quite rational and natural
applications to the alleviation of symptoms—com-
plexes of knowledge of general physiological properties and actions of plant, animal and mineral medica.
Notice, for example, the drugs cited to kill intestinal

worms and those to purge or stop diarrhoeas . . . the very small magical parts of the papyri ought not to be exaggerated.

When I last met Dr. Sobhy in Cairo he told me a story which I have reason to believe, since he has studied Ancient Egyptian medicine for many years; however, I have not had the opportunity of checking it from any other source. It is that in one of the medical papyri there is a prescription for the treatment of wounds or open sores. The ancient physician prescribes a certain type of *fungus* which grows on still water.

Penicillin in 2000 B.C.? Too fanciful, perhaps. But one never knows.

CHAPTER *12*

## BUYING AND SELLING

IT is afternoon. Two figures are moving down the long, dusty, crowded road to the dockside of Thebes. One is a tall, broad-shouldered Nubian, who holds firmly the hand of a small, excited boy. The lad points eagerly to right and left. He drags at his companion's arm, urging him to stay. Here is a man with a performing monkey; there a young girl dancing, surrounded by a circle of hand-clapping men who squat in the dust. Nearby a female contortionist gravely ties her supple limbs into knots. There are so many things to distract a small boy; but his tall companion walks resolutely on, looking neither to right or left. He dare not, for the small boy is Per-hor, son of the Vizier, and the companion is only the porter who keeps guard at the door of the great man's house. A trusted servant, he has been instructed to meet Per-hor at the school gate and escort him home, but the youngster has persuaded the Nubian to let him see the market.

When they arrive at the quays, two great ships which have brought corn from the north are being unloaded. The corn is intended for the treasury of Amun, and scribes sit vigilantly watching the unloading, and noting down the number of sacks as they are brought ashore on the backs of the sweating porters. But not all the corn is going to its official destination. The crews of the ships have each received a measure of corn as part of their wages and some are already haggling with the merchants who sit cross-legged on the quay with their jars and baskets. No coin is exchanged, for none exists. All trading is by barter.

Per-hor drags his guardian through the crowd, darting first to this side and then to that. Here is a fish dealer squatting before his rush basket. A woman tries to beat down the price. Nearby another tradesman has ointment to sell. Another offers small white cakes. A man offers a collar in exchange, but the cake seller refuses with a scornful wave of the hand. "Then take these sandals as well," says the prospective buyer, and the deal is made.[1]

Here sits another dealer with a basket of red and blue ornaments. Next to him another man is selling fishhooks. Brown-skinned sailors look down from the decks; one of them tosses a bunch of dates to a group of giggling girls.

Not one person in this great crowd of buyers and sellers receives cash wage or salary. All payments and transactions are in kind. The same system applies to the very top of the social scale. The great officials derive their wealth from the estates which they own or administer on behalf of the King, who is the greatest landowner. To us, with our elaborate banking and currency systems, such an arrangement seems primitive, yet the Ancient Egyptians did not find it inconvenient. They held markets, paid salaries, lent on interest and collected taxes without a coin changing hands. On the other hand, although a man might exchange geese for corn, cattle for timber, the relative value

[1] This scene is from a tomb at Sakkara.

of the goods would be assessed in terms of some common object of known value.

Under the New Empire one of the measures of value was a spiral of copper wire, called the *uten*. This measure became so firmly established that a spiral became the hieroglyphic sign for the *uten*. This does not mean that these copper spirals changed hands in the market, except perhaps to adjust some slight difference in value, but the value of objects of the most diverse kinds were related to them.

The servant Thothmes of the Temple of Thoth was presented with a bill by the tax authorities in which the value of each object was assessed in this way. Here is part of the assessment:

Skin, raw, 4 pieces, worth in copper 8 *uten*.
Skins, made up into coats of mail, 1 piece, worth in copper 5 *uten*.
Stick, prop-stick, inlaid work, 1 piece, worth in copper, 4 *uten*.
Hoe, worth in copper 2 *uten*. . . .

Erman, in his *Life in Ancient Egypt,* mentions another transaction in which 119 *uten* of copper were paid for an ox

. . . but of these 119 *uten* not one metal *uten* changed hands. A stick with inlaid work was substituted for 25 *uten*, another of less elaborate design for 12 *uten*, 11 jars of honey for 11 *uten*, and so on.

Another Egyptian unit was the *deben*, a word originally meaning "ring"; but after a time it appears to have come to signify not the object itself, but its weight or value. Similar units of value existed in other civilizations; the Chaldeans at one time seem to have used bars of metal, and among African and other primitive tribes today, beads and other objects of convenient size are used in similar fashion.

Internal trade within Egypt seems to have been on a relatively small scale. The reason is simple. Each *nome* was self-supporting, producing everything needed by its inhabitants. Each royal or priestly estate had its weavers, its brewers, its carpenters, and other craftsmen, and the peasants themselves grew the food which they ate. There can be no comparison with the complex industrial civilizations of our own day, when a housewife can enter a shop and buy products which come from all over the world. There was no need for merchants as we understand the name. Unlike the later Phoenicians and the Greeks, who were carriers and middlemen, the Egyptians supplied their own needs.

The only exception to this rule was in the field of foreign trade. At various times Egypt had a lively commerce with neighboring countries—sometimes, as in the case of Nubia, Syria, and Libya, with lands which had come under their control—but at other times with lands which were too remote for conquest, such as the Aegean islands and "The land of Punt" (Somaliland).

Nubia (the modern Sudan) was known to the Egyptians as far back as the Old Kingdom and possibly earlier. From time to time inroads were made into the country and its people forced to pay tribute. The kings of the Twelfth Dynasty were particularly active in this area, and one of the commonest representations in monuments is a line of Negro prisoners, their hands manacled and the women with children on their backs. From Nubia, either by trade or conquest, came ivory, ebony, gold, precious stones, and such exotic imports as ostrich feathers (for fans), ostrich eggs, monkeys, panthers, and giraffes.

These were mainly loot which went to swell the treasuries of Pharaoh and the Amun priesthood. But with other countries the Egyptians undoubtedly carried on trade. There was, for instance, the mysterious "land of Punt" of which the exact whereabouts are uncertain. Some writers have suggested that it may have lain on the west coast of India, but the generally accepted opinion is that it lay on the African coast to the south of the Red Sea, in the area occupied by modern Somaliland.

In the great temple built by Queen Hatshepsut (the predecessor of Tuthmosis III) at Deir-el-Bahri is a famous sculptured relief depicting in fascinating detail an expedition to Punt carried out under the Queen's direction. Much of it survives today just as it appeared to little Per-hor and Kenamun, and generations of young men in whom it must have stirred the lust for travel.

Erman's description of this relief cannot be bettered:

In one of the harbours of the Red Sea lies the fleet, which the soldiers of Her Majesty are to conduct to that distant country; the stately vessels are about 65 feet in length, and they are provided with thirty rowers and with gigantic sails, which stand out like wings beyond both sides of the ship. The great jars which contain the provisions are being conveyed on board by a rowing boat; on the shore, however, near the trees to which the ships are tied, a sacrifice is being offered to the goddess "Hathor, Lady of Punt" that "she may send wind." Then the sails are hoisted up, the sailors climb the yards to make fast the last ropes, the rowers dip their long oars in the water, and from the wooden partitions in the bows, in which the two captains stand, resounds the command, "To larboard." The ships begin to move, and thus "the royal soldiers voyage on the sea, they begin their beautiful journey to the Divine Land, and voyage happily to Punt."

Further along the wall another relief shows the arrival at Punt. The artist, who may have made the voyage himself, has depicted primitive huts built on piles, each with a ladder leading to a single door. These miserable dwellings, set among luxuriant tropical vegetation, aroused the contempt of the civilized Egyptians. The men wear skirts and have pointed beards and pigtails, just as they are represented in the reliefs of the time of Khufu, more than one thousand years earlier. As the Egyptians disembark, the men of Punt advance with suitable humility, led by their chief, whose huge wife suffers from elephantiasis. Her grotesque figure provides a butt for the cruel wit of the artist. The unfortunate woman, described satirically as "the princess," bulges out of her shapeless clothing, and behind her is an ass, under which an inscription reads: "The donkey which carries his wife."

Then trading commences. Up and down the gangplanks hurry the Egyptians, carrying ebony, ivory, "white gold from the country of Amu, sweet-scented woods, all manner of eye-pigments, baboons, monkeys and greyhounds, slaves and their children. Never has the like been brought to any king whatsoever since the beginning of time."

But the most important product of Punt is the incense for which the country is famous. Not only do the Egyptians carry back piles of incense, but numbers of growing incense trees are carried aboard, to be replanted in Egypt.

And what do the people of Punt get in exchange? On a table set up on the beach the delighted natives examine the goods which the foreigners have brought: gay necklets, daggers and battle-axes, besides bread, beer, wine, fruits, "and all good things of Egypt." All, one suspects, of considerably lower value than the products for which they are being exchanged.

The Egyptians, as we have seen, also had commerce with Crete and the "Isles of the Great Sea," and with Syria. Egyptian weapon makers traveled in the land of Retenu, selling their wares, and Semitic girls were often bought or taken as slaves.

Some of the objects imported into Egypt from Syria, and bartered for corn and other products, were ships, chariots, carriages, weapons, musical instruments, drinks ("the beer of Quede, the wine of Charu"), horses, bulls, cows, and other cattle.

But hardly any of this wealth reached the mass of the people. Most of it went into the storerooms of the King and the Treasuries of the Gods. Having no means with which to buy food, the Egyptian workmen were dependent entirely on the will of their masters for mere sustenance.

All, from the highest to the lowest, were ruthlessly taxed. Since the Egyptians had no monetary system, one might ask: How were these taxes gathered? With the peasants and the farmers, it was relatively simple: they gave up a portion of the produce of their land—their crops and cattle and the cloth which was woven and spun by their wives and daughters. But how were the numerous scribes and officials assessed and taxed?

These men owed their power and wealth to gifts bestowed by the king, *i.e.*, by the state. In return for his services, a high official might receive, as a mark of esteem and honor, a beautiful villa, a fine carriage, a splendid boat, numerous Negro and other slaves, besides cattle, food, wine, and clothing. The snag, from the official's point of view, was that all these gifts were *registered in his name*. When the taxgatherers made their assessment, they could estimate to a fair degree the extent and nature of the man's wealth, and taxed him accordingly.

The Ancient Egyptians, of all degrees of society, paid their taxes with no better grace than we do today, and there survive in documents numerous complaints of unfair assessment, extortion, and injustice.

Here is one, from a shepherd of the name of Thothmes, who had lost a donkey, on whose work he was to be taxed. Apparently, one Paere, who should have given it up, had kept the animal.

Channa, the officer of the company *Shining as the Sun* stationed in the country of D'aper, gave you a donkey and told you to give it to Thothmes. But you have not given it to me. Then I seized you when you were in Memphis with Amenmose the chief of the stable, and said to you, "Give it to me." You then said to me, "Don't take me to court; I have the donkey, but if you send to fetch it I will give it up." So you said, and you swore by the life of your lord that you would cause it to be brought to me. Behold, however, you have *not* sent it to me, and now they [2] demand from me the work of the donkey, year by year, while it has been with you.[3]

It appears, therefore, that we have little reason to envy the Ancient Egyptians, except for the fact that they had no income-tax forms to fill out!

[2] The tax collectors.
[3] Erman, *Everyday Life in Ancient Egypt.*

# CHAPTER 13

## THE PEOPLE'S PHARAOH

A GROUP of young girls is standing in a dim, pillared hall. Heavy black wigs of curled hair brush their bare shoulders. Pleated robes of fine, semitransparent linen hang to their sandaled feet. Their finger- and toenails are dyed with henna, and in their slim hands they carry *systra*. The girls are priestesses of Amun-Re, and their leader is Nofret, who has survived her illness.

The Vizier's daughter is glad to have recovered in time for this great occasion. All Thebes is *en fête*, for the Pharaoh Tuthmosis III, Menkheperre, King of the South and North, beloved of Amun, has returned in triumph after his victories over the Retenu. Yesterday Nofret watched his army march into Thebes. Today she waits within the Temple of Amun with the other priestesses to sing and dance before Pharaoh when he comes to the Temple to offer sacrifice.

In the sun-bright courtyard outside, ranks of shaven, white-robed priests are waiting expectantly. This is the inner courtyard leading to the pillared hall beyond which lies the sanctuary of the god. Only the priests are admitted within this enclosure, but there are other courtyards, surrounded by columns and colossal statues, each linked with the next by massive stone pylons before which pennons fly on tall masts. These are already packed with people, ranged in order of rank, and marshaled by officers carrying staffs of office. A broad lane has been left down the center to enable the King and his train to enter the Temple.

Outside, beyond the first pylon with its fluttering pennons, a broad avenue of sphinxes stretches in a straight line to the quayside. Stand on that quay and look to right and left along the river bank and you will see lines of troops —brown-skinned Egyptians with their spears and shields, coal-black Negroes from the Sudan, and foreign auxiliaries, such as the Shardana, wearing horned helmets. And behind them, talking, gesticulating, struggling to see over the backs of the soldiers, are thousands of common people. Every yard of the route along which the King will pass is thick with them.

Suddenly a mighty shout goes up. Far out across the sunlit river a great flotilla of boats is approaching: the royal barge, golden in the sun, the barges carrying the Court officials, the Royal Bodyguard, and the River Police. Menkheperre, the mighty conqueror, the scourge of Egypt's enemies, is once again coming to offer sacrifice to his father, Amun, bringing rich spoils of war to enrich the Temple of the King of Gods. This is the forty-second year of Menkheperre's reign. Seventeen times during those forty-two years he has led his armies out of Thebes, and seventeen times he has returned victorious. From Nubia in the south to the far-off Euphrates in the east, scores of petty kingdoms owe allegiance to Pharaoh, and the kings of the neighboring states, of Mittani and of Hittites, stand in fear of him.

> I myself have stretched out my two hands,
> I have bound them for thee. . . .

So Amun is personified, addressing Tuthmosis in a hymn of victory:

The earth in its length and breadth, Westerners and Easterners, are subject to thee.
Thou tramplest all countries, thy heart glad;
None presents himself before thy majesty,
While I am thy leader, so that thou mayest reach them,
Thou hast crossed the water of the Great Bend [1] of Naharin, with victory, with might. . . .

In the inner courtyard the great officials cease whispering and stand in nervous silence. Rekhmire fiddles with a gold armlet; the General Amenemhab adjusts his helmet; Nofret pushes back the curls of her wig. There is a distant shrilling of trumpets and the roar of the crowd is louder, so that now their cry can be heard:

"Life! Prosperity! Health! . . . Life! Prosperity! Health!"

The ranks of shaven priests look towards the great bronze gates, which stand open. They hear the tramp of feet, the sound of hoofs, the rumble of chariot wheels. The procession is entering the outer courtyard, where thousands prostrate themselves, their foreheads in the dust.

"Life! Prosperity! Health! . . . Life! Prosperity! Health!" shout a thousand voices.

Shadows fall across the bronze doors. The cavalcade is entering. First, ranks of priests in white robes, then officers of the Royal Bodyguard, marching slowly, their young faces set and unsmiling under their high, plumed

---

[1] The Euphrates.

headdresses, gold gleaming on their bare arms, their spear tips catching the sun; then the fanbearers holding huge ostrich-feather fans; and now, born aloft in a golden palanquin on the shoulders of twelve noblemen, the Pharaoh himself. With one movement, all except the priests and highest officials prostrate themselves.

The slim priestesses, led by Nofret, advance slowly, shaking their *systra* and singing:

"How splendid is he who returns in victory!
For Amun hath caused him to smite the princes of Palestine."

And the deep-voiced priests reply:

"All folk, all folk of the House of Amun are in festival,
For Amun-Re loveth the Ruler. . . ."

Tuthmosis III is a small man with a plump, unmilitary face. He is over seventy, but years of arduous campaigning have toughened his frame and hardened his features. His bare, sunburned arms are muscular, and his carriage is that of a younger man. He wears the tall double crown which has symbolized for fifteen hundred years the union of Upper and Lower Egypt. On his brow are the twin insignia of the Two Lands, the falcon and the serpent (see illustration on Plate 44). And in each strong hand he carries another symbol—the crook, representing Upper Egypt, and the flail for Lower Egypt. He wears a long skirt of fluted linen, and he is shod with golden sandals.

If we could be miraculously transported back to that time, if we could stand unseen, among the prostrate, adoring crowd

> . . . among them, but not of them; in a shroud
> Of thoughts which were not their thoughts

we would probably feel amused or indignant. Some of us would see only a pathetic little human being, in a hat too big for him, surrounded by ridiculous pomp, the creature of a corrupt court and a cynical priesthood who exploited the superstitions of the masses for their own selfish ends. That would be the Marxist analysis. And even the more tolerant among us would feel a sentimental pity for the toiling millions who built his monuments, labored in his fields, and shed their blood in his wars. "The Pharaoh's people," we would think. . . . "Poor devils."

But we would be wrong. That was not how the Ancient Egyptians felt about their king, and if we are to enter into their minds we shall have to make a considerable effort of the imagination.

In the first place, his function was fundamentally religious. He was a priest-king. He was the intermediary between the people and the unseen powers which controlled the fate of men. He was also the people's representative in a far more profound sense than that implied by the modern use of the phrase. The health and virility of the nation was embodied in that of the king. Thousands of years earlier, when civilization was beginning to develop in the Nile Valley, the king reigned as long as his physical powers lasted. When they began to fail, he was probably sacrificed, a custom which prevailed among other primitive peoples. With the passage of time this custom was abandoned, but a relic of it survived in what came to be called the *heb-sed* festival. At regular intervals—originally every thirty-three years—the king had to go through a ceremony in which he renewed his health and vigor.[2] Part of this consisted in offering at the altars of the gods of the northern and southern Kingdoms. In the time of Djoser, for example (2800 B.C.), the king had to run a fixed course, presumably to test his vitality, and one of the most beautiful carved reliefs in Djoser's Step Pyramid shows him performing this ritual sprint.

To the Ancient Egyptians, their king was not a human being but a god, the son of Amun-Re himself. He never died. He joined his father Amun; he "went to his horizon." Take the description of the death of Amenemhat I in "The Story of Sinuhe" quoted in Chapter IX:

> King Amenemhat flew away to heaven and was united with the sun, and the god's body was merged with his creator. . . .

Did the kings themselves believe that they were gods and the sons of god? I believe that they did. One has only to consider the effect of absolute power upon modern tyrants and then add to that the sanction of religion, and the effect of the sacramental atmosphere which surrounded the Egyptian kings from the cradle upwards, and it becomes impossible to believe otherwise.

[2] But later the ceremony was performed at shorter intervals.

The king was surrounded by ritual and symbolism. Every hour of his life was regulated by ceremony:

> Every hour was definitely allotted to various duties, to do something enjoined, and not to indulge in pleasures. On rising in the morning, the first thing was to read the despatches that had arrived, and this probably involved dictating the replies. Then came the ceremonial purification, the assumption of the robes and insignia, and proceeding to the sacrifice. Before that act the high priest, with the king and people standing around him, prayed for the health of the king, recited the praises of the king, and then a curse on all offences that had been ignorantly committed, laying the blame on the ministers. This must have been a considerable criticism of affairs, which, owing to the great power of the priesthood, would be hard to control officially; it is said that this was to guide and check the royal conduct. It is not stated whether the manual act of sacrifice was by the king or the high priest, but it was the king's ceremony, and he inspected the entrails. . . . He then finished the sacrifice, presumably the offerings of wine, oil, and other libations. Then followed the sermon, when the priests read edicts, laws and historical passages fitting for the time.
>
> The food of the kings is stated to have been plain and limited, which points to their being kept under regimen to preserve their health for the well-being of the country. In Africa, when a king shows weakening health, he is killed to prevent the country similarly suffering. It would appear that the Egyptian priest-

hood arose through the magician and the priest, and not from physical leadership. . . .[3]

When state trials were held involving members of the royal family, they were held strictly according to legal form, without the king's presence. He had, in fact, less real power than the Emperor Claudius or King Henry VIII. Nor did his responsibilities end with the death of his subjects. Just as in life he endowed them with land, so at their death he allowed them, for the future life, land for keeping up their tomb offerings. "Thus," says Petrie, "the king was the maintenance of his people during life by his vicarious position, and after death by his sustenance of them in the tomb."

I have often wondered if the zest which Tuthmosis showed for warfare, and his fondness for foreign campaigns, may have been due in part to his desire to get away from the cramping ritual of his office and express himself as a human being in the way he understood best—as a general.

Look at him now, as he sits, weighed down by his heavy crown, the royal serpent and falcon gleaming on his brow, the crook and the flail held against his breast in the position sanctioned by a tradition of more than two thousand years.

"Life! Prosperity! Health!" shout the Pharaoh's people. But as the bearers carry him on through the Hall of Columns to the dark sanctuary where he, as High Priest, must perform the sacred rites before Amun, Tuthmosis knows that he is the people's Pharaoh.

[3] Petrie, *Social Life in Ancient Egypt* (Constable).

The Pharaoh is offering sacrifice to the golden image of Amun in the holiest part of the Temple. Assisted by priests, one wearing the mask of a hawk in impersonation of Horus, the other in an ibis-headed mask of Thoth, the God of Wisdom, Tuthmosis opens the door of the sacred shrine, fumigates the statue with incense, sprinkles it with water from the sacred lake, presents it with its crown and insignia, and sets food offerings before it. The sanctuary is dimly lit by a small aperture in the ceiling. The chanting of the priests sounds faintly in the distance.

Meanwhile, like a glittering, many-colored snake, a great procession is coiling its way through the decorated streets of Thebes, moving slowly towards the Temple. Dust rises from the feet of columns of marching spearmen. Other regiments follow: archers with long bows slung from the shoulders, quivers swinging at their sides, Nubians carrying clubs, foreign auxiliaries, Libyans, Shardana, bearded Syrians. Then come the chariots in a long, glittering line, the horses adorned with nodding plumes of many colors and their harnesses burnished. An endless, undulating roar goes up from the massed crowds as the soldiers march by. Ox wagons, filled with booty, follow and columns of asses laden with the sack of cities—from Erkatu, from Tunip, from Kadesh, from Wawat—ornaments of gold and semi-precious stones; vessels of silver and gold; myrrh, incense, wine, honey. Then come cattle, bulls, bull calves, antelopes, gazelles, ibexes . . . and finally the human loot—hundreds of pitiful slaves, men and women, trudging along in the wake of the procession and guarded by soldiers.

But the principal prisoners are not in the procession. Seven or eight kings and princes of the subjugated lands wait in an antechamber of the Temple, their clothes stained and ragged, their hands fast pinioned behind their backs. Grim-faced Egyptian soldiers guard them while outside the crowd waits for Pharaoh to emerge from the sanctuary. These men, according to a long-established custom, are to be sacrificed to Amun.

The procession has halted; officers move rapidly along the ranks, shouting orders and marshaling their men. All is ready for the moment when the Pharaoh leaves the Temple to mount his chariot of gold and electrum to drive in triumph at the head of his victorious army.

One of the regiments of charioteers has drawn up near the entrance to the Temple. To it has been accorded the place of honor, for it has distinguished itself in battle. And in one of the chariots stand Senmut and Kenamun.

Senmut has recovered from his wounds, though they have left him with a permanent limp, and one side of his face is twisted. Bitterly he reflects that he has fought his last campaign. For Kenamun this should have been a moment of joy. He has been blooded in a tough campaign. He has seen action and acquitted himself well enough to earn promotion. But his pleasure is dimmed by sorrow for his friend.

"I wish they'd move," says Senmut, twisting the reins about his fingers and hitching at his belt.

"It's the moment of sacrifice," replies Kenamun.

"A barbarous custom," mutters Senmut, his face twitching.

"But it's the custom," Kenamun objects in a half-hearted manner.

Senmut turns on him savagely.

"There you speak like your father," he says. "It is the *custom*. Always in Egypt it is the *custom*. So our fathers did and so must we do."

"But the Asiatics would have done the same to us."

"Is that any reason why we should imitate the barbarians?"

Kenamun sighs, and then says, "It seems you don't like Egypt."

"You are wrong," replies his friend. "I do like Egypt. But is that any reason why I should approve everything that's done here? Not all the foreigners sacrifice their noble prisoners. The Keftiu do not."

"But they do, Senmut. Paibese told me that they sacrifice their prisoners to their god, a bull."

"Then Paibese is a fool. He means the bull-leaping, which is not the same thing."

"The bull-leaping?"

"Yes. The Keftiu train their prisoners to encounter the bull in the arena. They have to leap over its horns. But if they are brave and skillful, they can escape death. That is not the same as dashing out your prisoner's brains with a club. . . ."

A great and terrible roar comes from the direction of the temple. It is taken up by the crowd and spreads far and wide through the city. Senmut shudders. "It's over," he says. "Now perhaps we can move."

In the Hall of Columns the bodies of the slain chieftains lie in a pool of blood. Nofret and the priestesses shake their *systra*, and begin the Battle Hymn of Amun. Their thin, high voices echo from the lofty roof, mingling with those of the priests:

"I have come, causing thee to smite the princes of Zahi;
I have hurled them beneath thy feet among the highlands.
I have caused them to see thy majesty as lord of radiance,
So that thou hast shone in their faces like my image.
I have come, causing thee to smite the Asiatics,
Thou hast made captive the heads of the Asiatics of
   Retenu.
I have caused them to see thy majesty equipped with thy
   adornment,
When thou takest the weapons of war in the chariot. . . ."

Slowly the King is borne from the Temple on the shoulders of his bearers. The massed crowds prostrate themselves again as he mounts his war chariot and moves to the head of his waiting troops. Then, amid the shrilling of pipes, the clashing of tambourines, and the beat of drums, it begins to move.

Senmut jerks the reins.

"I'd like to go to Keftiu-land," he says.

# CHAPTER 14

# HOUSE OF ETERNITY

AUTUMN has come, and with it the inundation. Far, far to the south, the waters of the Blue Nile, swollen by rains, are rushing into the main stream, bearing a rich treasure of fertilizing mud from the mountains of Abyssinia. But the ancient Egyptians have never heard of Abyssinia, or the Blue Nile. For them the world ends south of Nubia, and the life-giving flood, the yearly miracle, comes as the gift of Re. At Thebes and other towns along the serpentine length of the river, the priests are studying the "nilometers," measuring the level of the floodwater and comparing it with those of previous years. It is a "good Nile" this year, and already scribes are calculating the expected yield of the land, and the amount of taxation which can be levied. The river began to rise two months ago, in August, when the Egyptians held the High Nile Festival. Last month, September, it was at its highest. Now it is October and in a few weeks the river will begin to subside, and sowing will commence in November.

A strange stillness broods over the imperial city. Where, a few months ago, there were green fields stretching to the foot of the limestone hills, there is now a lake-like expanse of water. You can take a boat from the quayside on the eastern bank and land within a short distance of the Necropolis on the western side. Many of the peasants are idle, but some have been recruited for work on the monuments. Big boats are arriving from distant Assuan loaded with granite, and in the Temple of Karnak, work is being done on the reconstruction and extension of the building. Gangs of sweating men haul on ropes, grunting a rhythmic chorus as a 600-ton obelisk is slowly raised into position.

It is early morning. Boats move continually across the broad, brown river, their sails throwing long shadows which point towards the western cliffs. The voices of the boatmen come clearly across the water, and somewhere a pipe plays plaintively.

In one of the boats, a big, handsome craft with gilt mountings, sit Rekhmire and his wife, Meryet. They are going to visit Rekhmire's tomb, his "House of Eternity," which has been hewn out of the western cliffs in preparation for the Vizier's death. There is nothing unusual in this. Men of rank spent as much time and care on the preparation of their eternal homes as they did on their earthly dwellings, for life is short and death is long. And "home" is a much more accurate description than "tomb," because the Egyptian planned his sepulcher as the everlasting dwelling place of his *ka,* or spirit.

These tombs vary in size according to the wealth and importance of their owner, but they have certain features in common. There is a deep shaft leading to the sealed burial chamber, in which lies the embalmed body. There is a chamber containing the statues of the deceased and usually his wife, facing the offering chamber or chapel in which the relatives of the dead noble make food offerings for his spirit. The statue, which accurately represents the dead man as he appeared in life, is intended as a dwelling place of the spirit when it leaves the body to partake of the offerings. The walls of these chambers, as described in an earlier chapter, are covered with paintings or sculptured reliefs representing the activities of the dead man in life, which he wishes to continue in the afterlife. There are also sacred texts to assist him when he appears in the Judgment Hall of Osiris, and representations of his relatives making their offerings, which by a process of sympathetic magic will become real should his descendants fail in their duty.

The boat glides to the landing stage. The Vizier and his wife disembark; servants assist them into carrying-chairs, and in these they are carried up the slope towards the cliff face. On their way they pass through the many-streeted town in which live the embalmers, the coffinmakers, the carvers and painters, the makers of funerary furniture, and the priests whose duty is to make regular offerings at the tombs. Through one open doorway they see gilded and painted coffins leaning against a wall. This is a coffinmaker's showroom, in which relatives of the dead may choose the design which best pleases them. Within are also tables set out with miniature mummy cases which serve the same purpose. Nearby are the embalmer's booths, temporary structures which are erected for each person to be embalmed, and dismantled afterwards when the work is complete. From one booth comes the strong smell of natron from the natron baths in which the bodies are soaked for the requisite number of days.

It takes seventy days to complete the full process of embalmment and mummification, but there are quicker and cheaper methods. In fact, the embalmers will offer you

223

a choice of three alternative processes, according to how much you wish to pay. Here are descriptions of the three methods, beginning with the most expensive:

First they draw out the brain through the nostrils with an iron hook, taking part of it out this way, the rest by pouring in drugs. Next, with a sharp Ethiopian stone, they make an incision in the flank, and take out the entrails, and after cleansing the body and scouring it with palm-wine, they purify it with pounded incense; then, having filled the body with pure pounded myrrh and cassia and other perfumes—frankincense excepted—they sew it up again. Having done this they soak the body in natron, keeping it covered for seventy days, for it is not lawful to soak it for a longer time than this. And when the seventy days are accomplished they wash the corpse, and wrap the whole body in fine linen cut into strips, smearing it with gum, which the Egyptians use instead of glue. After this the relatives, having taken the corpse back again, make a wooden case of human shape, and, having made it, place the corpse inside and, having closed it up, put it in a sepulchral chamber. . . .

For those who desire the medium style to avoid heavy expense, they prepare the corpse thus: Having charged their syringes with cedar oil, they fill the inside of the corpse without making any incision or removing the viscera, but inject it at the anus. Then they close the aperture to prevent the liquid from escaping and soak the body in natron for the pre-

scribed number of days. On the last day they let out
the cedar oil which had been previously injected, and
such is its potency that it brings away the bowels and
internal parts in a fluid state, and the natron dissolves
the flesh so that nothing remains but the skin and
bones. When this has been done, they return the body
without further manipulation.

The third manner of embalming is this, which is
used only for persons of slender means: After washing
out the body with a purgative they soak it in natron
for seventy days and deliver it to be taken back.

That was how Herodotus described the process in the
fifth century B.C., but the methods were traditional and
had been in use for thousands of years. The bodies of men
and women of the Eighteenth Dynasty were embalmed in
a similar manner.

As Rekhmire and Meryet mount the slope towards the
tombs in the cliffside, they stop to allow a cortège to pass
them. First come servants carrying alabaster jars containing food and precious unguents; then come men carrying
long wooden chests containing the ornaments and clothes
of the dead man. A sled follows, dragged by two men; inside this are the canopic jars containing the embalmed viscera which have been removed from the body. Before it
strides a lector priest, chanting solemnly. Other priests accompany the body itself, the mummy resting on a couch
beneath a canopy with the whole mounted on another sled.

"In peace, in peace, unto the Great God," cry the
priests as the procession passes. Behind them come the fam-

ily and their friends, and a group of professional women mourners, who weep and tear their hair, beating their breasts and sending up the old wailing cry for the dead.

The Vizier and his wife watch the cortège as it passes out of sight round a projecting bastion of rock; then they signal to the carriers, who lift the chairs and carry them up the steep path to the tomb entrance.

In front is a courtyard 60 feet wide; behind it the cliffside has been smoothed flat, forming an imposing façade to the tomb, the tall entrance to which is exactly in the center. The foreman of the workmen comes to greet his lord, falling on his knees and touching the ground with his forehead. Then he rises and stands respectfully on one side as the nobleman and his wife pass through the entrance. As it is early morning, the sun streams directly through the doorway and lights up the interior, so that the hundreds of figures seem to march along the plastered walls; the reddish-brown skins of the men, the pale cream complexions of the women, the white robes, the gold of their ornaments, the blue, green, and red of their jewels seem to glow with an unearthly light.

To help the illusion, the foreman has caused bronze mirrors to be placed at an angle to right and left of the entrance, so that not only is the east-west passage opposite the entrance illuminated, by the direct rays of the sun, but the transverse passage which opens out to right and left is also lit, by reflected light.

The tomb is, in fact, T-shaped, the crossbar of the T running parallel with the face of the cliff, the long arm of the T stretching from the entrance for more than 100 feet into the hill. This narrow passage is like a funnel, relatively low at the entrance, but the roof slopes upwards at a fairly steep angle till it reaches the far wall at a considerable height above the entrance. And high on that wall, just below the painted ceiling, is a niche, within which rest lifelike statues of Rekhmire and Meryet, seated, with Meryet's arm placed affectionately around her husband's waist. The effect is startling, particularly at this moment when the sunlight streams full onto the figures.

At the far end of the hall workmen perched on scaffolding are applying color to the designs which the draftsmen have left. Others are carefully painting in the hieroglyphic texts which describe the scenes. While Meryet is critically regarding her statue, her husband is examining the texts which describe his appointment as Vizier, on the south side of the wall. There sits Tuthmosis, wearing his tall crown and clad in the cerements of Osiris. In front of him stands Rekhmire, with his titles above him. The text reads:

The guiding principles enjoined on the Vizier Rekhmire; the assembling of the council at the audience hall of Pharaoh—life, prosperity, and health to him!—and causing the newly appointed Vizier to be brought in.

His Majesty said to him, "Look thou to the hall of the Vizier and be vigilant over all the procedure in it. Lo, it is the consolidation of the entire land. Lo, as to [the position of a] vizier, lo, it is not pleasant at all; no, it is bitter as gall. [Lo] it is the bronze which surrounds the gold of the house of its [Lord]. Lo it is to have no consideration for himself or for the officials of the magistracy, and not to make slaves of the general public. Lo, as to all that a man does in the house of his lord he speaks approvingly. Lo, what he does is not . . . for any other man.

"Lo, if a petitioner of Upper or Lower Egypt, [that is] the entire land, come, prepared for the court . . . to hear [his case] thou shalt see well to it that all the procedure is in accord with what has legal sanction, that all the procedure is in accord with due regularity. . . .

"Lo, whenever an administrator hears cases let there be publicity, and let water and air report about all that he may do. Lo, then, his conduct is by no means unperceived. If he does anything [unseemly] and he is to blame he is not to be reinstalled on the authority of an acting official but men shall learn of it on the authority of his [proper] judge. . . ."

Meryet, bored by the long text which her husband has begun to read, has wandered into one of the transverse rooms. Here the workmen are just putting the finishing touches on a scene depicting a family feast. There sit Rekhmire and Meryet, larger than life-size, with their guests. A little band of musicians plays, and the words of their song are set down beside them:

[Put] balsam on the locks of Ma'et, for health and life are with her . . . ! O Amun, the heaven is uplifted for thee; the ground is trodden for thee; Ptah with his two hands makes a chapel as a resting place for thy heart. Come, O north wind! I saw thee when I was on the tower.

In another scene, two women and two young girls, the daughters of Rekhmire, hold out to him the *systra,* which he touches. The text says:

> The enjoyment of the sight of good food, music, dancing, and song, anointment with oil of balsam and unction with olive oil, lotus held to the nostril, bread, beer, date wine, and dainties of all sorts, presented to the *ka* of the seigneur, mayor of the city, Rekhmire, his heartily loved wife, mistress of his house, Meryet, being with him [see illustration on Plate 47].

In a lower picture one of Rekhmire's sons, Amenhotep, and two of his brothers, offer flowers, saying:

> "Enjoyment, glad exultation, and participation in good food, summer lotus for the nostril, and [oil of] balsam suitable for the crown of the head, for the *ka* of the seigneur, mayor of the city, and Vizier, Rekhmire, and his wife, Meryet."

The graceful young girls place flimsy collars round the necks of the ladies, and pour wine or beer into their cups with the murmur:

> "For thy *ka!* Spend a festive day!"

And a group of three women, who are beating time to the music while they accept drink and ointment, remark:

"Can it be Ma'et in whose face there is a desire for deep drinking?"

Then Meryet is joined by her husband, who leads her to another part of the passage to admire a scene which depicts him inspecting the temple workshops of Amun. There are the jewelers drilling beads, the makers of alabaster vases, the carpenters making inlaid wooden cabinets, the leatherworkers, the ropemakers, the sandalmakers. And there too, much larger than his workmen, is the Vizier himself leaning on his staff with his train of forty retainers.

This noble, who lays down principles and guides the hands of his workmen, making furniture of ivory and ebony, *ssndm* wood, *mrw* wood, and true cedar from the summit of the mountain slopes of Lebanon.

There are the metalworkers also casting the bronze doors for the Temple of Amun. The artist has just finished this scene, and looks to the Vizier for his approval. Rekhmire is satisfied, not only with the picture, but with the accompanying text, which reads:

Bringing Asiatic copper which His Majesty carried off from his victory in the land of Retenu, in order to cast the two doors of the Temple of Amun at Karnak, overlaid with gold which gleams (?) like the horizon of heaven. It was the Mayor and Vizier Rekhmire who directed it.

Now the couple return to the main hall, where the statues stand. On the north end wall is the Vizier's family history, with the names of his uncle, Woser, who was also a Vizier, and other ancestors. Here Rekhmire and Meryet are shown seated at table, while their son Menkheperre-Sonb, "Scribe of the temple dues of Amun," dressed in a leopard skin is consecrating their food. Another son, Amenhotep, is there too; Kenamun is not shown, though he appears in another picture. But three of the daughters are there: Ta-kha'et, Mut-Nofret, and Henet-towy.

Opposite, covering the length and breadth of the south wall, is an enormous inscription describing in full detail the appointment of Rekhmire to the Vizierate: he is careful to flatter the King.

When a second day had dawned and the morrow was come, I was summoned again into the presence of the good god, Menkheperre—may he live for ever— even Horus, the victorious bull appearing gloriously in Thebes. Now His Majesty knows what happens; there is nothing at all of which he is ignorant. He is Thoth in every respect. There is no matter that he has ever failed to discern. Every affair . . . he is cognisant of it like the Great Lady of writing. He changes the design into its execution like the god who ordains and performs.

So His Majesty opened his mouth and spake his words before me: "Behold, my eyes send me to my heart [for as much as My Majesty] knows the decisions are many and there is no end to them, and the judgement of cases never flags. Mayest thou act according as I say; then will Ma'et rest in her place." He admonished me very greatly: "Armour thyself; be strong in action; weary not; accuse evil. . . ."

Then follow thousands of words of what seems to us like self-appraisement; but we should do the Vizier an injustice if we accused him of mere vanity. He has his share of it, like most men who have reached great eminence, but now, in his tomb inscriptions, he is not boasting before men, but trying desperately to justify himself before the gods of the Underworld:

> I judged [poor and] rich alike. I rescued the weak from the [passionate] moment of the infuriated. I restrained weeping by replacing [it with] an avenger. I defended the husbandless widow. I established the son and heir on the seat of his father. I relieved the old man, giving him my staff, and causing the old women to say, "What a good action. . . ."

Meryet takes her husband's arm affectionately. The sun is rising, the tomb is becoming hot and stuffy, and she wishes to leave. But the Vizier lingers for a few more moments to study a painting which shows him receiving the tribute of the foreigners.

Here is a procession of Asiatics, men from Retenu whom Tuthmosis has vanquished. The porters carry—and the inscriptions describe—ingots of copper, jars of olive oil, gold and silver rings, lead, timber, chariots, and horses. The text reads:

> The arrival in peace of the chiefs of Retenu and all the lands of Further Asia in deferential obeisance, their tribute on their back, in the hope that there

would be given to them the breath of life because of loyalty to His Majesty; for they have seen his great victories—yea, his terribleness has dominated their hearts.

Now it was the father and favourite of the god, the confidant of the King, the Mayor of the city, the Vizier Rekhmire, who received the tribute of the various lands. . . .

There are men from Punt, men from Nubia, and men from Crete (Keftiu-land) and other islands of the Mediterranean. The Vizier and his wife look curiously at the paintings of the curling-haired, slim-waisted men of proud bearing, carrying the rich and lovely products of their country —the gold and silver vases; the tapering gold cups, elaborately wrought; the bulls' heads in gold; the richly ornamented arms which were more beautiful than the products of Asia (see illustration on Plate 48). Rekhmire has met their ambassadors, and he knows that they come as friendly traders, as representatives of a free and equal state, unlike the men of Pharaoh's dominions. Still

. . . It was the confidant of the sovereign, the mayor and Vizier Rekhmire, who received the tribute. . . .

Glancing down from the figures, Meryet says, "I wonder where Senmut is. . . ."

"He should be passing the Delta by now," replies her husband, leading her from the tomb.

For Senmut, through the influence of Rekhmire, has

been sent on an Embassy to the far-off island which few Egyptians have ever seen. The restless young officer, unable any longer to gratify his lust for travel by warfaring in Syria, has found another outlet. He is on his way to Keftiu-land, and perhaps Egypt may never see him again.

The sunlight stabs their eyes as they leave the tomb. They seat themselves in their carrying-chairs and are carried down the path, past the city of the workmen, and so to the riverside. As they climb into their barge again, Rekhmire looks at the bank and notices the watermark left by the subsiding river. He nods towards it and remarks to Meryet, "It's beginning to go down." The tackle creaks, the sail spreads lazily in the slight breeze as the boat moves back across the Nile towards Thebes. The Vizier settles himself under his awning and looks across the dazzling water towards the city.

So it all begins again. Soon the fields will be uncovered, and the sowers will be moving across the black mud, singing as they scatter the grain. Then the black expanse will give way to a haze of green, and before long the reapers will be out with their curved sickles, harvesting the crops. He had seen it all so many times. He had shown it in his tomb:

> Rekhmire . . . born of Bet and begotten of the *w'b* priest of Amun, Nefer-weben, son of the Mayor and Vizier, Amotu, enjoying the sight of the cows, delighting in the work of the fields and beholding the work of the seasons, summer and winter. . . .

And the servants cry:

"Accept the good produce . . . and eat, O Mayor and Vizier, a happy beginning, a happy day, a happy year, free from evil. . . ."

"Son of Nefer-weben. . . ." His father had been only a humble priest of Amun when he, Rekhmire, was born. Could the old man have been a prophet and seen his son's great destiny when he named him Rekh-mi-Re—"Wise as God"? It was a pleasing thought. Yes, the gods had been good to him.

Yet greatness had brought its cares. "Lo . . . [the position of a] vizier, lo, it is not pleasant at all. . . ." An exaggeration, of course, but there were times when he felt a slight nostalgia for his carefree youth, when, like Senmut, he had traveled abroad as a youthful official. Senmut . . . he wondered how he would fare in the land of the Keftiu? He, Rekhmire, would like to have seen it, but it was too late now.

As for the future, who could tell? He still hoped for many years of life, but the King was old, and when he went to his horizon, and a new king took his place, who knew what might happen? There had been more than one instance of great officials who had fallen from their high office when a new king sat on the throne of Pharaoh. But that was for the gods to decide.

His arm stole around the shoulders of his wife. Yes, life had been good. He had had many children, and seen some of them rise high in the favor of the King. His tomb was prepared, and every provision made for his welfare in the life to come. He had served the King well, and the King knew his worth:

He saw to it that the chapel of my tomb should last me for ever. He saw to it that my name should be stable therein, lasting and secure for millions of years, and that my memory should be lasting therein for ever and ever.

## FACT OR FICTION?

WHEN I began to write this book, I had no definite idea of what form it would finally take. My purpose was to depict as vividly and realistically as I could the daily life of the Ancient Egyptians, in the following order: their religion; their administrative system; the houses they lived in; their pastimes and recreations; the status of their womenfolk. I wished to add specific details of their varying lives in chapters dealing with education; the life of the laborers and craftsmen; the professions of soldier, doctor, and lawyer; literature; and the function of the Pharaoh in relation to his people. And in order to avoid producing a mere catalogue of facts, I decided to present this material in a semifictitious framework, although I knew that this method, though attractive, was difficult and a little dangerous in that it might lay me open to the criticism that I was not presenting history, but fantasy.

Therefore, I would like to assure readers who have read this book mainly for factual information that the bulk of the material is completely factual, and that where I have invented scenes and characters, they are based almost entirely on known and recorded incidents. To reassure them still further, I will now separate the facts from the "imaginative reconstruction."

Rekhmire was a real person. So was his wife, Meryet, his daughters, Mut-Nofret and Ta-kha'et, and his sons, Menkheperre-Sonb, Amenhotep, and Mer-y. All their names are given in the tomb, together with that of Kenamun, though archaeologists are uncertain whether the latter was a son or grandson. The first-named three sons were priests or officials, but Kenamun's occupation is not given, which is why I made him a soldier.

All that is known of Rekhmire is contained in his tomb inscriptions, which describe in great detail his functions as a great administrator. Nothing of his domestic and social life is known save that he gave banquets and parties, which are illustrated and described in his tomb, as in those of other Egyptian officials.

Apart from the voyage described in Chapter II and Rekhmire's visit to the Tomb in Chapter XIII, every incident I have described in the life of the Vizier is based on his tomb inscriptions. Nothing is known of the lives of Mut-Nofret, Ta-kha'et, and Kenamun, but all the incidents in which I have involved them could have happened. To take a few examples: Ta-kha'et's garden party is based entirely on the love poem, "The Trees in the Garden"; the hunting party at which Senmut and Kenamun are present is based on tomb paintings and descriptions; the boy Per-hor is imaginary, but young sons of the nobility did attend schools attached to the temples, and the school exercises are contemporary. Kenamun's adventures in Syria are fictitious, but based on contemporary documents describing the Pharaoh's Asiatic campaigns. The officer Amenemhab, who arranged for Kenamun to go to Syria, was a real person. His tomb can be seen in the Theban Necropolis, in which he describes the deeds of valor which he performed. He claims to have been first into the breach at the taking of Kadesh in year 42 of Tuthmosis's reign. He was a favorite of Tuthmosis III and his wife was the royal nurse. And another example is Nozme's getting drunk at the party—there are several illustrations of drunken female guests in the tombs, including one being overcome by the final stages of nausea.[1]

The young man Sinuhe, the lover of Ta-kha'et, is fictitious; so is Senmut, but the details of his military career are taken from those of other officers. Even his appointment as ambassador is not improbable. There is a record of an officer of chariotry who later represented his country at a foreign court.

Some readers may object that the views he expresses are out of harmony with conventional Egyptian ideas. To this I can only reply that history is not wanting in examples of young men who were ahead of their time. I can point to the Pharaoh Akhnaten, who, only a short while after the life of my hero, began a religious and aesthetic revolution, abolishing at one sweep the worship of Amun and hundreds of lesser gods, and substituting the veneration of one deity—the "Aten." He also seems to have been strongly influenced by Crete—the "land of the Keftiu"—to judge from the art which he encouraged.

Nofret's role of priestess is highly probable. It was customary for the daughters of the nobility to perform this office; the Queen herself sometimes acted as High Priestess, the "Bride of Amun." Nofret's illness, too, is

[1] One guest is recorded as saying, "Behold I wish to drink until I am drunk. My inside is like a straw!"

credible, and as for the "cure," there are many examples in the medical papyri of charms and spells to drive away fever. There is one which runs:

> Run thou out, O disease! Son of a disease! Who breakest down the bones, destroyeth the skull, disturbest the brain, and dost cause to ache the seven openings in the heads of the Followers of Horus, who turn to Thoth! Behold, I have brought the remedy against thee, the potion against thee, even the milk of one who has borne a boy, and odorous gum! May it force thee out! May it force thee out! May it drive thee forth! Come forth upon the ground! Rot! Rot! Rot! Rot! [2]

In this case a drug is indicated, but often only charms were used.

The wars of Tuthmosis III are well documented in the *Annals,* and the triumphal processions to the Temple of Amun are depicted on the temple walls. In the same inscriptions the King is shown personally dashing out the brains of captive chiefs with a club. There is some doubt as to this act being real or symbolic. At some period of Egyptian history it was certainly real. Equally barbarous acts are depicted in inscriptions of a later period than that of Tuthmosis III. For example, one of the Rameses is shown returning in triumph to Thebes with seven Syrian chiefs hung head downwards from the prow of his ship. I have assumed that such sacrifices were still made in the time of the warrior-king Tuthmosis III, though whether the King himself performed them is open to doubt.

[2] Shorter, *Everyday Life in Ancient Egypt.*

At the same time, the Egyptians were not as cruel as
the Assyrians and other Oriental peoples. For example, the
customs of killing the servants of a king and burying them
in his tomb was abandoned early in Egyptian history,
*shawabti*-figures statuettes being substituted. The ritual
killing of a king when he became unfit to rule was also
replaced by the *heb-sed* ceremony; and there are other
examples. These, and the humane laws set down in the
tomb of Rekhmire, also incline me to believe that men of
Senmut's character were not unknown in Ancient Egypt,
and that therefore his protest against such a barbaric survival is credible.

Readers may like to know what happened to Rekhmire
in his later years. A little is known. He survived Tuthmosis
III, living on into the reign of his successor, Amenophis II.
There is a scene in the tomb showing the Vizier making a
voyage down the river to meet the young King, who was
returning to Thebes when his father died, after a reign of
fifty-four years. The scenes continue with the succession
of Amenophis II, and then come to a sudden end, sug-
gesting a tragic close.

Whether or not the Vizier fell from office during the
lifetime of the new Pharaoh is not known, but it may well
have happened. Throughout the tomb a systematic attempt has been made to obliterate Rekhmire's name and the
figures of himself and his wife wherever the spoilers could
reach them. This was the usual fate of an Egyptian tomb
when its owners' enemies triumphed. His body has not
been found. Mr. de Garis Davies, whose beautiful volumes,
*The Tomb of Rekhmire at Thebes*, should be read by all
who are interested in this period of Egyptian history,
writes:

241

In the corner of the court near the left end of the façade there is a small burial-shaft (which may or may not be contemporary) giving access to a chamber to the south. Six other burial shafts have been sunk within the tomb; but none of them has yielded any trace of burial furniture belonging to the original occupants. Either, then, the place of interment of Rekhmire is still undiscovered, or exceptional care was taken to destroy every aid to his survival into eternity, even the protection of the gods in their temples, where he must have left memorials, being refused him. Such bitter malice seems unlikely when one notices how incomplete was the destruction of his memory on the walls of the tomb. Apparently burial in Thebes was denied him; perhaps he was exiled to some remote part of Egypt and interred there.

But in spite of the mutilations and the neglect and damage which the tomb has suffered in three thousand years, it is perhaps the most impressive and interesting example of a nobleman's tomb of the New Empire. When I revisited it in 1953 and saw the fine work of restoration and cleaning done by the Egyptian Government's Antiquities Department, I resolved to make the Vizier the central character of my book. I hope I have not done him an injustice.

May I say respectfully to his *ka*, "Now let thy heart be glad, O noble, and all thy affairs be fortunate!"

# BIBLIOGRAPHY

Baikie, James: *Egyptian Antiquities in the Nile Valley*. London (Methuen & Co., Ltd.). 1932.

Bouquet, A. C.: *Comparative Religion*. New York (Penguin Books, Inc.). 1950.

Breasted, J. H.: *Ancient Records*. Chicago (University of Chicago Press). 1906–1907.

———— *The Development of Religion and Thought in Ancient Egypt*. New York (Harper & Brothers).

———— *A History of Egypt*. New York (Charles Scribner's Sons). 1943.

Budge, Sir Wallis: *The Literature of the Ancient Egyptians*. London (J. M. Dent & Sons, Ltd.). 1914.

Clarke, S. and Engelbach, R.: *Ancient Egyptian Masonry*. Oxford (Clarendon Press). 1930.

Cottrell, Leonard: *The Bull of Minos*. New York (Rinehart & Company, Inc.). 1958.

———— *The Lost Pharaohs*. New York (Holt, Rinehart and Winston, Inc.). 1961.

de Garis Davies, Norman: *The Tomb of Rekhmire at Thebes*. New York (Egyptian Expedition Publications, Metropolitan Museum of Art).

Drioton, Etienne and Lauer, Jean-Philippe: *Sakkarah: The Monuments of Zoser*. Cairo (Institut Francais d'Archeologie Orientale). 1939.

Edwards, I. E. S.: *The Pyramids of Egypt*. New York (Penguin Books, Inc.). 1952.

Elliot-Smith and Dawson: *Egyptian Mummies.* London (George Allen & Unwin, Ltd.).

Engelbach, R.: "Mechanical and Technical Processes," Chapter Five, *The Legacy of Egypt.* New York (Oxford University Press). 1942.

Erman, A., and Blackman, Aylward: *The Literature of the Ancient Egyptians.* London (Methuen & Co., Ltd.). 1927.

Erman, A.: *A Handbook of Egyptian Religion.* London (Constable and Company, Ltd.). 1907.

—— *Life in Ancient Egypt.* New York (The Macmillan Company). 1927.

Evans, Sir Arthur: *The Palace of Minos.* London (Macmillan & Co., Ltd.). 1936.

Faulkner: "Egyptian Military Organisation," *Journal of Egyptian Archaeology,* Vol. 39.

Frankfort, H.; Wilson, John; and Jacobsen, Thorkild: *The Intellectual Adventure of Ancient Man.* Chicago (University of Chicago Press). 1946.

Gardiner, Sir Alan: *The Attitude of Ancient Egyptians to Death and the Dead.* Cambridge (Cambridge University Press). 1935.

—— *The Chester Beatty Papyrus.*

—— *Topographical Catalogue of the Private Tombs of Thebes.* London (B. Quaritch). 1913.

Glanville, S. R. K., ed.: *The Legacy of Egypt.* New York (Oxford University Press). 1942.

Herodotus: *History* (translated by Rawlinson). London (J. M. Dent & Sons, Ltd.).

Lucas: *Ancient Egyptian Materials.* New York (Longmans, Green & Co.). 1926.

Mercer, S.: *The Religion of Ancient Egypt.* London (Luzac and Co.). 1949.

Murray, Dr. M.: *The Splendour That Was Egypt.* New York (Philosphical Library, Inc.). 1949.

Petrie, W. M. F.: *The Building of a Pyramid in Ancient Egypt.* London. Part II, 1930.

——— *Social Life in Ancient Egypt.* London (Constable and Company, Ltd.). 1923.

Shorter, Alan W.: *Everyday Life in Ancient Egypt.* London (Sampson Low, Marston & Co., Ltd.). 1932.

Sobhy, Dr.: *Lectures in the History of Medicine.* Cairo (Fouad University Press).

Weigall, A.: *The Glory of the Pharaohs.* New York (G. P. Putnam's Sons). 1923.

# INDEX

# Index

# Index

# Index